for:

in S6-1.

# Conspiracy Series
# Volume 1

Moon Landings and 9/11

Conspiracy

2 Books in 1

Searched by:
K. Nugent #250.
on 01/03/20.

Shocking Conspiracy Series

Phil Coleman

# Table of Contents

# MOONSPIRACY REAL OR FAKE?

The Truth Behind The Moon Landings
Conspiracy Theories...

Shocking Conspiracy Series

Phil Coleman

# Introduction

Recently I had the privilege of speaking to a man of 71 who saw the film on TV of the Apollo 11 landing on July 20, 1969. He was at the time a young man who was a student at university studying science and mathematics.

He remembers the black-and-white images of that event very well. He describes what he saw as a seminal moment in his life.

He recounted how everything seemed very slow and how some of those who he was with said," This is so boring." He said he felt inspired when he heard the words of Armstrong about one small step for man and one huge step for mankind.

It sent a shiver down his spine and brought tears to his eyes. I too was deeply touched personally when I heard what was written on the plaque they left on the lunar surface.

This said in simple words that man first came to the moon in July 1969 and came in peace for all humanity.

I think we all yearn for peace and this extraordinary gesture, such a long way from our planet, so frequently driven by hatred and war, summed up all our yearnings.

My friend recounted how during his childhood and adolescence he had followed the space race with fascination and excitement.

The launch of Sputnik, how his parents had bought him a balloon toy modeled after the Sputnik, the Vanguard failures, the flight of Yuri Gagarin, the suborbital flight of Alan Shepard, John Glenn's orbit on Friendship 7 and all the many space exploits leading up to July 20, 1969.

The tragic death of Grissom and two others in 1967 was mentioned as a source of sadness.

This same sadness was felt by anyone who watched the explosion which destroyed the space shuttle Challenger in 1986.

Such sadness returned when the space shuttle Columbia disintegrated on reentry to the atmosphere in 2003.

He said that the Space Race had made a pleasant escape from the ever-present threat of the Cold War which hung over the whole world like a wet blanket.

A wet blanket which every so often got very worrisome when there was a crisis such as the Cuban missile drama in 1962.

We discussed the fact that apparently many people doubted whether the events shown rather indistinctly on an old television in 1969 had ever occurred.

The man said there may be doubters of this but he was not one of them. He felt that the doubts raised were ridiculous.

Probably done to make money for those who espoused them.

He said he had his doubts about 9/11 and about Pearl Harbor but none whatsoever about the Moon landing. In his opinion, the Moon landings were the real deal.

He deeply applauded the actions of astronaut Buzz Aldrin who punched conspiracy theorist Bart Sibrel for calling him a liar and coward.

Apparently, Aldrin who flew 66 combat missions in Korea and shot down 2 enemy planes found that accusation a bit rich.

My conversation with this man stopped at this point with me thanking him for sharing his thoughts about the events of half a century ago.

Events, which still reverberate within him. My parents have passed away so I cannot question them about the Moon landings however they never expressed any doubts to me that the Moon landings might be hoaxes.

As an author, I have to keep an open mind. This book will have a look at the evidence for and against the Moon landings.

It will be up to you the reader on the basis of what you read in this book and elsewhere to decide.

If you Google you will get many hits on flying saucers and astronauts. It would seem that there are astronauts who are as convinced as many others that there are alien civilizations out there.

There are estimates that the number of civilizations to be as high as 100 million. Given the vast size of the universe, it is no wonder that there is confusion as to the number of civilizations there may be out there. No one really knows.

If you check these sites you will find unconfirmed reports of Apollo 11 astronauts, Armstrong and Aldrin, seeing UFOs during the first Apollo mission to the moon.

There are conversations from various Apollo landings from the astronauts to central control and back again which have been construed by some people as evidence of an unknown civilization that has been on the Moon.

I will not be investigating this seriously in this book. As with the moon landings, I have to keep an open mind.

It is very unlikely that humanity is alone in the cosmos. Many books have been written and many side scientific papers published about this. This book only mentions these phenomena in passing.

This book considers conspiracy theories, what they are and why they occur.

It has a look at the backdrop to the whole Moon program, which was the Cold War. It outlines the Space Race of which the Apollo landings were the final episode then it moves on to the question of whether the moon landings were faked or whether they actually occurred.

It concludes with an examination of the future space travel of mankind.

Onto chapter 1.

# What Are Conspiracy Theories?

There are a vast number of websites dealing with a plethora of such theories. We shall propose in this chapter that this fact and the existence of Social Media such as Facebook and Twitter have made conspiracy theories far more prevalent and widely believed today than ever before but first.

**What are conspiracies?** A conspiracy is when two or more people get together and collude in order to commit an act, which is illegal, immoral or secret.

Criminal acts are often the result of conspiracies. Security agencies such as the

CIA and KGB concoct plans, which have to be confidential and are continually conspiring.

Companies usually desire to maintain commercial confidentiality but often employ people to infiltrate the confidentiality of others and in so doing act conspiratorially which means participate in a conspiracy.

Most people have been involved in mild conspiracies such as two children who collude to raid their parents' liquor cabinet. There are other conspiracies committed by governments which may or may not be successful. Here are two conspiracies, which were very successful.

**The location of the D-Day landings:** Long before June 6, 1944, the Allied Supreme Command had decided to invade France in Normandy and devoted all their planning to this end. They were very determined that the opposing Nazis would not know this.

The Nazis were certain that the invasion would occur in the Pas de Calais region of France which was much closer to Britain.

Although the invasion was not immoral it was certainly secret. The Germans did not realize they were wrong until it was too late.

**The rapprochement between China and the USA**: For some time before President Nixon's stunning visits to China in February 1972, there had been secret meetings between diplomats of these two great countries.

The planning for the visit whose consequences are still being felt was very secret. There was a conspiracy, even if it was not for immoral reasons.

Some conspiracies do go wrong though.

**Gulf of Tonkin Incident:** The Gulf of Tonkin Incident in 1964 involving US Navy ships and the North Vietnamese was a strange incident.

President Johnson of the USA used it as a pretext for a massive increase in the American involvement in the Vietnam War.

Planning for this involvement had been underway previously and kept secret.

This was a conspiracy, which resulted in the only defeat that the USA has had in a war. It was a disaster.

**Watergate:** The Watergate conspiracy is regarded as the largest political scandal anywhere in the world.

Basically, it involved a conspiracy between President Richard Nixon and some of his top aides to get subordinates to break into the US Democratic Party's national committee headquarters in the Watergate complex in Washington in 1972.

The intruders were caught and over the next two years, the extent of the conspiracy was discovered. This discovery led to the resignation of President Nixon in 1974.

**Kathleen Kane:** In 2016 the Attorney General of Pennsylvania Kathleen Kane was convicted on a number of charges including perjury and criminal conspiracy.

She had leaked information for a grand jury in order to discredit a political rival. She was caught and lied about what she had done however her downfall was decided by a jury thus ending a brilliant career.

**What are Conspiracy Theories?** There are many definitions of what a conspiracy theory is.

The best I have found is the online encyclopedia Wikipedia. It is a good idea to read their definition.

A conspiracy theory is a belief that things should not be taken at face value. The reason being that there are very powerful people or forces who are directing events for their own reasons such as financial gain or power.

Conspiracy theories have always existed. Perfect examples are the ideas promoted by the Nazis that the Jews were responsible for Germany's defeat in World War 1 and what the Nazis believed was the decay and ruin of the Aryan race.

Another was that promoted by the Communists that every wrong thing in society could be attributed to monopoly capitalists who controlled everything and masterminded oppression, poverty, and war so as to reap profits.

Another far more widespread belief is that there is a fallen angel called Satan who is the unseen ruler of the Earth and all who live in it and is responsible for all evil.

This belief is at the root of most religions.

**What Are Some Widely Believed Conspiracy Theories?** The murder of the US President JF Kennedy is officially believed to be the work of a lone gunman Lee Harvey Oswald.

This explanation is seen as a cover-up by many who see the President's death as the result of the machinations of the Cubans, the Mafia, the Teamsters, Vice President Johnson or the Illuminati.

Princess Diana, divorced wife of Prince Charles, was killed in a motor smash with her lover Dodi Fayed in a car driven too fast by Henri Paul, a security official of Fayed.

Since then Diana's death has been blamed on conspiracies involving the British Secret Service MI6, the Royal Family, and the Illuminati.

On September 11, 2001, passenger planes seized by Arab terrorists belonging to Al

Quaeda crashed into the Twin Towers in New York.

As a consequence of this President Bush justified an invasion of Iraq which caused much trouble throughout the world.

This event has led to countless conspiracy theories most of which allege official coverups. Once again the Illuminati feature among possible conspirators.

**Who Or What Are The Illuminati?** The Illuminati actually existed and were a secret society which was founded in Bavaria in the 18th century. They were banned during that time and later blamed for the French Revolution.

Since then they are alleged to have been responsible for most wars, revolutions, atrocities and catastrophes.

They have metamorphosed, in the minds of their believers, into a sinister group who wish to build a New World Order.

This group of people is alleged to include the Kennedys, the Onassis family, the Rothschilds and even Angela Jolie and Lady Gaga.

Some of the people believing in this conspiracy allege that members have to commit blood sacrifices.

It is believed by some adherents that such famous people as Michael Jackson, John

Lennon and Elvis were killed by the Illuminati.

The Illuminati are alleged to have various symbols which include such things as 666, a double lightning bolt which was the SS Nazi symbol, the pentagram, and the skull and crossbones.

Another symbol of the Illuminati is claimed to be the all-seeing eye on the pyramid which is featured on the US dollar.

**Why Do Conspiracy Theories Spread So Quickly?** Conspiracy theories seem to be more prevalent these days. If you go into any bookshop you will see books and magazines which question and contradict the official version of many things.

Any surfing of the Internet will produce thousands and thousands of similar such refutations of orthodoxy.

In 2016 the Americans elected a man as president who seems to believe in such theories. Conspiracy theories are especially prevalent when people feel threatened and they find that others, particularly those in power give voice to their fears.

There is solid research to show that although the belief in conspiracy theories is not more now than it was half a century ago the rate at which conspiracy theories form is much quicker. The cause of this is new technology.

There are countless millions of people throughout the world using their smartphones and tablets to put pictures and videos of events online, in other words, they are supplying news.

There are probably, even more, people exchanging opinions and views with one another on this news.

The combination of these two phenomena, unheard-of in human history before, has led to the proliferation of conspiracy theories that is seen nowadays.

**What causes Conspiracy Theories?** The phenomenon of conspiracy theories has been the subject of many scientific studies.

Many of these reach the conclusion that there is in human nature a desire to search for patterns.

Some of the greatest scientific and mathematical achievements can be attributed to this.

Programmers working in artificial intelligence create code which does exactly that on things called perceptrons which look for patterns.

Their search for these is reinforced by the use of rewards and punishments so that the execution of the code is similar to the training of a dog.

Once people see a pattern then the next step is to presume that this pattern is the result of an agent who created the pattern.

This behavior had great value in evolution and in the early days of mankind when humanity was in the hunter-gatherer phase.

A noise that was heard by an early human might just be the wind or it could be a saber tooth tiger.

The safest course of action was to always presume a saber tooth tiger was responsible.

The noise was the pattern and the saber tooth tiger the agent in this particular case.

Like the programmer successfully coding his or her artificial intelligence program the response has been programmed into our DNA.

Nowadays we find our agents in the form of the government, the Illuminati, the deities of religion and other things once we have seen a pattern.

Nowadays we all have good reason to be suspicious of the actions of government, big business, bureaucracies, academia etc.

It is quite natural to see one of them as an agent rather than accept the explanation they give.

**Can any harm result from Conspiracy Theories?** Most conspiracy theories are harmless nonsense.

If someone chooses to believe that the Illuminati are behind the ills of this world in order to establish World Government then such a belief is probably harmless.

Unfortunately, not all conspiracy theories can be dismissed as harmless nonsense.

There is a theory that vaccines cause autism.

This theory insists that children are being injected with a poison that could cause them to have autism.

The reason that this is done is to make profits for the drug companies, which produce the vaccine and have influenced the government to force the vaccines upon an unwary public.

As a consequence of this belief, many

parents prevented their children from being vaccinated. There is solid research to show that autism is not caused by vaccines.

However, if a child is not vaccinated against measles or some of the other diseases which he or she could be vaccinated against they could well lose their lives.

No parent wants that for their son or daughter. The effect of withholding vaccination from them puts them in much greater danger than if they were vaccinated.

This is a clear-cut case where belief in a conspiracy is harmful.

**Is The Moon Landing The Subject Of Conspiracy Theories?** To those who believe the Moon landings were real they represent the summit of human achievement.

The Extraordinary organization, brilliant technology, great courage, indeed the Moon landings represent everything good and noble that mankind is capable of.

Others though do not believe the landings took place. They believe it was impossible in 1969 to send and land a man on the Moon.

They are sure NASA faked the landings by making films purportedly showing something that did not occur.

They believe that NASA did this under directions from the government who wanted to convince the world that America had better technology than Russia.

They are certain there has been a cover-up of the facts for at least half a century. Yes, the Moon landing is the subject of conspiracy theories.

Amazingly the Illuminati have been insinuated into this by some but most see a more mundane reason.

The reason that the government would want to do this is the Cold War. The next chapter will discuss this extraordinary episode in history.

# The Cold War

*"I grew up during the Cold War when everything seemed very tenuous. For many years, right up until the fall of the Berlin Wall, I had vivid nightmares of nuclear apocalypse."*

—Justin Cronin

The Germans launched a carefully planned invasion of Poland on September 1, 1939, and so began World War II.

Russia, or the USSR as it was then, also invaded Poland on September 17, 1939, and seized the eastern half of that tragic country.

A country that has been the subject of so many invasions over the centuries.

The Soviets invaded Poland because of the Ribbentrop-Molotov pact of August 1939. In this pact, Nazi Germany and Soviet Russia agreed on the mutual invasion.

In reality, Russia invaded Poland as they needed as much territory between them and the Germans as they could get.

They realized the Nazis would eventually invade them.

For similar reasons they absorbed the three small countries, Lithuania, Latvia and Estonia, adjacent to them on the Baltic Sea in early 1940, and also launched an attack on Finland in 1940.

On June 22, 1941, after conquering most European countries the Germans, at last, launched a massive attack on the USSR.

For nearly six months the German army or Wehrmacht could not be stopped. The Russians suffered millions of casualties.

However, the Russians repulsed the Germans during December 1941 in the battle of Moscow.

In that same month Hitler, the German dictator, declared war on the USA. This was to prove a fatal error for the Nazi regime.

The Nazis renewed the offensive against the Russians in 1942 with spectacular victories. The Russians were in full retreat.

However they recovered and inflicted a catastrophic defeat on the Wehrmacht (German Army) in the battle of Stalingrad.

At the end of 1942, the Nazis were retreating, both in Russia and North Africa.

The Germans suffered another very serious defeat in the battle of Kursk during mid-1943 and were never again on the offensive on the Eastern Front against the Russians.

All they could do was retreat and suffer defeat after defeat as they did so. For another two years or so the war continued until Hitler committed suicide and the Germans surrendered in May 1945.

During their conquest of the Nazis, the USSR had taken over the countries of Eastern Europe. The Russians forced these countries to turn communist and the Iron Curtain fell over Europe.

What is called the Cold War between the communists and the West began.

The Cold War was not a war in which the armed forces of the Soviet Bloc and the West clashed but a state of hostility none the less.

The only actual shooting wars were by proxy in the Korean War, in colonial wars and revolutions, often, but not always started by the Communists, against corrupt regimes, such as the Batista regime in Cuba.

There were some incidents which seemed to threaten war such as the building of the Berlin Wall in 1961, the Cuban Missile Crisis of 1962 and wars in the Middle East. However, actual war between the West and the Soviet Bloc never happened.

Germany was completely smashed by invasion and by bombing. The USSR set up a communist regime in East Germany.

The biggest German city, Berlin, was surrounded by this communist state. The isolated democratic enclave in the middle of a communist dictatorship was a major problem for the communists.

The USA, the UK and France were to have free access to West Berlin. The Russians tried to stop this by imposing a blockade of Berlin in 1948.

The blockade was lifted by a huge Allied airlift. The Cold War deepened, as China became Communist in 1949.

The Russians were terrified the USA would use the atom bomb against them. The atom bomb had brought the war against Japan to a close in August 1945.

The Russians as a result of spying and a massive effort acquired the atom bomb in 1949.

At the end of the Second World War in Europe, the Allies found that the Germans were far more advanced in rocketry than Britain, the USA or the USSR.

They had devastated parts of London in 1944 with the V1 rocket and had developed a weapon of far greater potential with the V2 rocket.

The Americans were deeply impressed and immediately took as much of the German rocket program back to the USA as possible.

As well as actual rockets they took as many German rocket scientists as they could.

One of these scientists, Wernher von Braun, played a key role in the development of what became the US space program.

The operation to bring the German rocket program to the USA was called Operation Paperclip. In some cases, a blind eye was turned on war crimes these people may have committed.

All combatants on the battlefield had used rockets with great and in some cases devastating effect during the war.

The British and Canadian armies used the Land Mattress rocket launcher in the final stages of World War II.

The United States army had little use for rocket launchers except for a few rocket launchers mounted on tanks however their navy used them with great effect to bombard Japanese positions in the Pacific War.

The Japanese used them in the later stages of the Pacific war in the Philippines, Iwo Jima, and Okinawa.

The Russians used the Katyusha rocket launcher which was called the Stalin organ against the Germans from 1941 onwards until the end of the end of the war.

The Germans also had a rocket launcher which was similar to the Katyusha and they often used it.

During the Second World War, the Germans developed a very powerful flying bomb called the V1. The V1 obviously came before the V2. Its effect was far more serious for the British than the V2.

The Germans rained thousands of V1 bombs upon London and caused a lot of damage as a result. The V1 was the precursor of the cruise missiles, which are used in the 21st century.

Like the V1 the cruise missile does not go terribly fast but is very accurate and also very devastating. Both the Americans and Russia have deployed them with great effect in Syria.

The Americans saw great possibilities of equipping huge rockets with atomic payloads if the German V2 could be developed and improved further.

This motivated their actions in moving the German rocket program to the USA as soon as possible.

The Russians also saw this possibility and as a consequence there developed a continuing improvement in rocketry on both sides that saw both the USA and the USSR develop what are called ICBM rockets.

ICBM stands for intercontinental ballistic missile. These missiles were developed so that they could not only be launched from land-based silos but also trains and even nuclear submarines.

Not only did the Americans and Russians have these but also the British and French. The rockets were improved to the extent that one missile could carry several atomic warheads.

Missiles with this capability were called MIRVS. MIRV stands for multiple independent reentry vehicles.

Another factor in the Cold War was the relationship between Communist China and the Soviet Bloc. The Chinese worked independently of the other countries and acquired the atomic bomb in 1964 and a nuclear missile in 1966.

Although the relationship of both the West and the USSR with China is of great importance in the Cold War it had little impact on what follows.

Another crucially important factor in ending the Cold War was the complete collapse of communism throughout the world during the period of the 1980s and early 1990s.

Although of great importance this event occurred long after 1969, which was the year of the Moon landing, alleged or otherwise.

As this book is about the Apollo moon landing and whether or not it occurred some readers may wonder why a chapter has been devoted to the Cold War.

The Apollo enterprise was extremely expensive and it is unlikely it would have occurred had it not been for the Cold War.

It was the Cold War that provided the

rationale for what is called the Space Race between the USA and Russia.

If it had not been for this tension between the West and the Soviet bloc it is unlikely that the Apollo missions would ever have occurred.

The Cold War kept on providing justifications such as the building of the Berlin Wall, the Cuban Missile Crisis and the South East Asian Wars for the Space Race.

Both America and Russia saw their exploits in space as demonstration of the superiority of their technology. Both saw the Space Race as a way of proving to the world that their social system was best.

In the end, the outcome of the Cold War was not decided by the Space Race but by other things.

It has been said that the outcome was decided because 'blue jeans and the Beatles' were far more appealing to the youth of the Soviet Bloc than class war, ethnic music and promises of a golden future, which never came.

The next chapter will describe the history of and what happened during the Space Race.

# The Space Race

Today's space rockets are among the greatest of humanity's many achievements. They result from the work and development of many thousands of years.

Currently, rockets are the only means we have of going into space. In the second decade of the 21st-century, efforts are afoot to change this, as you will find out in the last chapter.

When were the first rockets? By 100 A.D., the Chinese had gunpowder. They used this to power the first rockets.

It is doubtful if the first Chinese dabblers in rocketry had any idea of how their innovation would affect world history hundreds and thousands of years into the future.

The first military use of rockets was by the Chinese who stuck these rockets onto arrows, which were fired by archers.

It did not take long to find arrows were not necessary and rockets were on their way. Their uptake was not universal or guaranteed at this stage.

During the earlier part of the thirteenth century, there was a war between the Mongols and the Chinese. In one battle, the Mongol were defeated by the Chinese who used a lot of these simple rockets.

For historians of rocketry, this was a display of their potential, although it is doubtful that the combatants in that ancient battle realized this.

As is so often the case with weapon systems, the Mongols made rockets for their own use and it was probably from them that Europeans initially learned about rockets and their potential as a weapon.

During the next two hundred years, developments in rocketry were seen in a number of European countries, including Italy, France, and England.

Newton established his Three Laws of Motion in the final part of the seventeenth century. His laws completely described force and motion in situations of low speed.

These laws were the scientific foundation of modern rocketry. With these laws, rockets could be developed in a systematic way.

Development took place all over Europe for use in war. They were used to great effect by the British against the United States in the 1812 war. The rockets used had great success in devastating American strongholds.

Until the end of the First World War, there was no major role for rockets in the bloody battles of that dreadful combat as high-power artillery was far more effective in inflicting damage on enemies.

They were first used by the French in the

battle of Verdun in an air to ground role. The British used them against German airships but these were not particularly successful.

It was in Russia in 1898 that a man called Tsiolkovsky with great foresight made the suggestion of space exploration using rockets.

A short while later it was he who suggested the use of liquid fuel for rockets. If that were used the distance the rocket traveled could be greatly increased.

In the early twentieth century, there was a brilliant American named Robert Goddard who had a great interest in rockets. He did much work with them and as a result of his efforts; the capabilities of rockets were greatly improved.

The Second World War saw rockets come to be seen as a powerful weapon. The Germans suffered a great shock in 1941 when the Katyusha rocket system called Stalin organ was used by the Russians in the Battle of Moscow.

These proved to be formidable weapons; the Germans were so impressed that later they developed and used similar weapons.

In their island-hopping campaigns of the Pacific War, the Americans used rocket systems of this type fired from landing craft.

With much larger rockets the Germans were well ahead of the Allies and built a powerful rocket called the V2. Sadly for them, it appeared too late in the war to prevent their defeat.

Wernher von Braun, the leader of the program that developed them, went on to lead the space program of the Americans during the 1950s and 1960s.

As World War II ended the Cold War began. This featured the world's two great superpowers fronting against each other.

From the late 1950s onwards space became another area of this competition. Each country made every effort to prove that its technology, it's military, and its economic system was better.

By the middle of the 1950s, the Cold War was a major feature of life in most countries. It was driven by an arms race and the ever-increasing threat of atomic weapons, and by spying between the two systems.

These tensions were prevalent throughout the period 1946-1989. They were made worse by such events as the Berlin wall in 1961, the Cuban missile crisis in 1962 and the Vietnam War.

On October 4, 1957, a Russian missile launched Sputnik the first artificial satellite and the first object made by man placed into the Earth's orbit. This day marked the beginning of what is called the Space Race.

The leadership of the USA was shocked by this and introduced many changes to their education system. One of these changes was an innovation called the New Math.

The New Math was a peculiar idea promoted by some educationists. It was believed that if primary school and secondary school students were taught abstract algebra and other advanced concepts then they would be able in the future to compete with the Russians.

This idea was adopted over the next couple of decades throughout the Western world and was a total disaster.

The launch of Sputnik was a very frightening surprise to the Americans. They realized that rockets of the type, R-7, which had launched Sputnik, might be used to launch nuclear warheads against the USA and her allies.

It was very important that the Americans did not get for too far behind the Russians.

In 1958 America launched its first satellite, which was called Explorer 1. It was built by the US Army under the direction of the German rocket scientist Wernher von Braun.

During 1958 President Eisenhower set up NASA, the National Aeronautics and Space Administration.

President Eisenhower also set up a means by which orbiting satellites could be used to get intelligence on what the Russians and their allies were doing.

In 1959 the Russians managed to land their first vehicle onto the moon. It was called Lunar 2.

In April 1961 the Russian cosmonaut Yuri Gagarin was the first person to orbit the Earth traveling in a spacecraft that was called Vostok 1.

It was not until 1961 that the Americans were able to put a man into space. A man called Alan Shephard, who ventured into space on May 5 of that year, although he did not go into orbit, did this.

Later in May 1961, President Kennedy stated that the United States would land a man on the moon before the end of that decade. The program to build the lunar landing system was called Project Apollo.

In 1962 John Glenn, who eventually became a senator and died in December 2016, became the first American to actually orbit the Earth.

He was the fifth person in space. He did so in the Friendship 7 spacecraft.

From 1961 until 1964 the budgets of NASA was increased by 500%. There were as many as 34,000 NASA employees and 375,000 employees who were working on some aspect of the space program in America.

Apollo had a very serious setback in 1967

when three astronauts were killed when a spacecraft set on fire during a launch simulation.

During this time the lunar landing program of the Soviet Union proceeded very slowly, due to internal debate over its importance and the death in January 1966 of its chief engineer who was called Sergei Korolev.

Slowly but surely the Americans pulled ahead in the Space Race. In December 1968 Apollo 8 became the first manned space mission to orbit the Moon.

Apollo 8 was launched from the huge facility that NASA had developed in Cape Canaveral, Florida.

Finally, in mid-July, 1969 the US astronauts Michael Collins, Edwin Aldrin and Neil Armstrong launched from Cape Canaveral on Apollo 11 and successfully made a landing on the lunar surface, in other words, the Moon.

With this landing, the United States was victorious in the Space Race - A race that had begun with the launch of Sputnik in 1957.

The Russians made four unsuccessful attempts to launch lunar landing craft between 1961 and 1972. There was a Launchpad explosion in July 1969 that was very serious.

After the lunar landing in 1969 there were another five landings then the emphasis of the space program became shuttles, satellites, unmanned flights into space and space stations.

It is only recently that a return to the Moon has been suggested.

The next chapter examines the actual Moon landing. It briefly runs over the events leading up to this landing. A landing that many believe never took place.

# The Moon Landing

We have seen that as World War II ended it
was realized by both the USA and the USSR
that the Germans were far more advanced
than any of the Allies in the development of
rockets that could be used in war.

The Americans who were developing the
atomic bomb, something the Russians
probably did not know, saw enormous
possibilities in the putting of such a bomb on
a V2 rocket and were very keen to get their
hands on the V2 for this purpose.

Realizing that their erstwhile ally was now
their enemy both countries actively recruited
German scientists and engineers who had
worked on the Nazi rockets. The American

effort to do so was called Operation Paperclip.

In this operation, 1600 Germans were brought to the USA and put to work developing rockets, which might be used for military purposes.

The Russians also actively recruited German scientists and engineers and took 2200 of them at gunpoint back to the Soviet Union.

The Germans who went to America were put to work in the New Mexico desert at the White Sands testing ground further developing the V2 rocket. The project to develop the V2 in America was called Project Hermes.

The first V2 firing was on April 16, 1946, and some 60 flights later the last of the V2 flights was launched on October 29, 1951. It was found that rocket components which were stored for long periods deteriorated so many of those brought to the USA from Germany were unusable.

The Americans learned while experimenting with the V2, how to manufacture their own rockets. They also learned much else that would be of inestimable importance in the decades, which followed. They had greatly improved on the original V2's, which came from Germany.

From this project arose a series of US rockets that included the Corporal, the Redstone, the Aerobee and the Atlas. It was realized at this time that the conquest of space would be a powerful way of demonstrating the superiority of a social system.

In 1952 the International Council of Scientific Unions named the period of July 1, 1957, until the end of 1958 as the International Geophysical Year as a result of strong solar activity during that period.

In October 1954 this same union called for the launching of artificial satellites to perform various activities. The commission wanted satellites to map the surface of the earth.

During July 1955 President Eisenhower announced plans to launch an American satellite. The rocket chosen was the

Vanguard rocket in preference to the Redstone rocket, which was primarily being developed for military purposes. In 1957 the Soviets launched Sputnik 1 and the space race began.

The Americans tried to launch Vanguard but it failed miserably on both the first two times it tried to put satellites into orbit.

An alternative was found in the Explorer project, which was headed by Wernher von Braun and involved the Redstone rocket which had been designed under his leadership. Wernher von Braun had tried to get this rocket adopted at the time the decision was made to go with the Vanguard.

The Vanguard program was continued and was successful on three occasions. There were a total of eleven attempted launches.

In January 1958 the Americans finally launched a satellite with the Explorer 1 aboard a Juno rocket. Explorer 1 was used to do some very important scientific research.

Explorer 1 discovered magnetic radiation belts around the Earth that were named after the brilliant scientist James Van Allen. Explorer 1 stayed in orbit until 1970.

The details of the Space Race were set out in the previous chapter. It was pointed out that the launching of Sputnik galvanized American efforts in space.

In addition to the renewed efforts they made in space, there were concomitant changes in other spheres such as education. As was mentioned these were not as successful as in space.

The Americans who were to fly into space were called astronauts, Russians were called cosmonauts. These words were terms derived from Argonaut.

The astronauts were a very elite group of men. President Eisenhower decided that the military could provide all the men who were to travel to space.

From the initial group of less than 100 outstanding candidates, only seven were chosen. The seven chosen did not include the three who eventually went to the Moon on Apollo 11.

Many astronauts were trained in a special astronaut school run by Chuck Yeager. Yeager was an amazing military pilot.

He was a veteran of World War II during which war he shot down 11 German planes. Later he flew in combat both in Korea and Vietnam.

In addition, he was a test pilot who was the first person to fly faster than the speed of sound in a level flight. He also piloted a test rocket plane with near fatal consequences.

Of the three who went to the Moon on Apollo 11, all were fighter pilots with two,

Armstrong and Aldrin, being veterans of the Korean War. They both had outstanding records in that war.

President Kennedy was elected in 1960 and initiated the program to land an American on the moon by the end of the 19 Sixties in May 1961.

This gave rise to the Apollo program that had its first launch in October 1961 of a Saturn rocket. He announced the decision to initiate the program which led to the Moon landing before a joint session of Congress.

Kennedy was under great pressure to demonstrate that the USA could catch up to the Soviet Union in space. The Russians had consistently been ahead of the Americans in space up to this point. The Americans did not realize at this time that this success could not possibly last.

He also needed something positive to counter the very bad publicity he was getting over a disastrous military setback, the failed Bay of Pigs invasion of Cuba.

As a consequence, we can say that Cold War considerations played an extremely large part in the making of this momentous decision and announcement.

Saturn rockets were to be the first stage of all of the subsequent Apollo missions. The first payload was just water.

There followed many tests of various facets

of the program. The rockets used were Saturns of increasing size and power.

The reason for this is that the heavier the payload the bigger the rocket required. In order to develop the speed to escape the Earth's gravitational pull a very large quantity of fuel has to be taken.

The weight of fuel required is an important factor in calculating the size of rockets.

During this sequence of tests, there was a terrible tragedy on January 21st, 1967. In this disaster the Apollo command module, which was being tested exploded into fire, killing the astronauts Gus Grissom, Roger Chaffee and Ed White.

As we shall see in the next chapter some believe their death was no accident. They are convinced it was murder authorized by people in high positions of authority.

They did this in order to prevent the astronauts from revealing the Apollo program to be a gigantic fraud.

Despite this tragedy, the Apollo program continued leading to three missions testing Apollo before the trip to the Moon in July 1969.

Apollo 8 took men around the Moon in the command module, which was the part of Apollo containing humans.

Apollo 9 tested the lunar module in an Earth

orbit. The lunar module was to make the descent to the moon from the command module.

Apollo 10 was the dress rehearsal before the actual landing. In this mission, the lunar module descended to about 8.4 miles from the surface of the moon.

The command module, called Columbia, was one of three parts of the Apollo spacecraft which were projected into space by the huge Saturn rocket. It housed the astronauts.

Apollo also contained the lunar lander or module, which was called Eagle and the service module. The service module contained the engine and the consumables for the trip.

Finally, we come to the actual Moon landing. On July 16, 1969, at 9:32 AM Apollo 11 launched from the Kennedy space Center at Cape Canaveral, Florida, with astronauts Collins, Aldrin and Armstrong as crew. Armstrong was the commander.

Scores of thousands of people physically witnessed this extraordinary event in Florida as it unfolded.

Six hundred million more watched on television, the largest TV audience for any event up to that time. An audience not exceeded until Prince Charles wed Princess Diana in 1981.

The flight took 76 hours and covered 240,000 miles as the Apollo traveled from Earth to the Moon. Apollo moved into orbit about the moon on July 19. At 1:46 PM on July 20 Aldrin and Armstrong left Apollo in a craft called the lunar module, named Eagle.

There was a computing system on board Eagle. The computing power of modern smartphones far exceeds that onboard the Eagle. The computing file of the guidance system was a tiny 64kb!

Two hours later the Eagle descended to the moon and alighted in an area of the Moon called the Sea of Tranquility. After landing Armstrong broadcast to Mission control in Houston," the Eagle has landed."

Six hours later Armstrong opened the hatch of the lunar module and descended via a ladder.

Millions of people were watching on TV at the moment when he stepped down onto the lunar surface and said his famous words, "that's one small step for man, one giant leap for mankind."

A short time later he was joined by Aldrin. They planted the flag of the USA, performed some scientific experiments and spoke with President Richard Nixon. About three hours later they returned to the lunar module.

The lunar module was about one and a half tons in weight. It was in two stages, one a descent stage, the other an ascent stage.

Armstrong and Aldrin slept on the surface of

the Moon inside the module and on the next day they returned to Apollo.

Armstrong and Aldrin were on the Moon for 21 hours including two and a half hours on the lunar surface.

On July 22 Apollo began its return to Earth. On reentry, the material of the outer shield burnt up as the craft was entering the Earth's atmosphere. This was quite deliberate and was done in order to protect those inside the capsule.

The three astronauts splashed down in the Pacific on July 24, 1969. On the return, all three astronauts were held in quarantine for 21 days.

The reason for this was the unlikely event that during their visit to the Moon they had been infected in some way, which would spread a contagion to humanity.

Following this mission, there were another five successful moon landings and another, which was aborted due to technical problems.

The longest lunar landing was Apollo 17. The astronauts were Eugene Cernan and Harrison Schmidt. They stayed on the lunar surface for three days.

The Apollo program that successfully landed men on the Moon was very expensive. In today's dollars, the cost was around $100 billion.

It was also very labor intensive and employed at least 400,000 people. Since late 1972 no human being has been to the moon.

Many people believe that the events described in this chapter never took place and that human beings have never been to the moon.

They believe that the entire program to put humans on the moon never occurred. They believe there was a conspiracy to convince the world that an event had occurred when in fact it had not.

This will be looked at in detail in the next chapter.

# Evidence for a Fake

Most historians regard July 16, 2009, as an important day for humanity. Nearly fifty years have gone by since the U.S. astronaut Neil Armstrong, closely followed by astronaut Buzz Aldrin, became the first human beings to set foot on the moon.

Yet there are numerous people who still believe the Apollo 11 moon landing was an elaborate fabrication and hoax. Here are some of the claims against the landing.

**Claim 1:** It is possible to tell that Apollo was almost certainly faked on the grounds that the American banner appears to be fluttering and waving as though "it was being blown in the wind" in recordings and photos from the landing.

However, as far as nearly everyone knows the airless, lunar surface has absolutely no atmosphere and hence could not possibly provide the wind that would cause the fluttering of the Star Spangled Banner!

**Claim 2:** The reflections of Neil Armstrong and the lunar module used to land on the lunar surface, the Eagle lunar lander, are seen with great clarity in the visor of Buzz Aldrin in one of the most famous photographs during the July 1969 landing on the Moon.

You can easily see that Apollo was a hoax in light of the fact that only two space travelers walked on the moon in this landing, yet in this and other photos both can be seen. However, there is absolutely no indication of a camera.

The question has to be asked," who took the photo?" Did it take itself miraculously? Or was there another person present to take the photos in a film studio? Is this evidence of a fake?

**Claim 3:** Dave Bowman, the main actor in the 1968 film Arthur C. Clarke's Space Odyssey: 2001 was terribly excited in the film by the vastness of space and the myriad of stars.

His words in the film made an indelible impression on its viewers as to how human visitors to outer space should react.

Their disappointment was great when the Apollo astronauts did not express themselves with the same exuberance as Bowman.

Some felt this lack of excitement was yet further proof that Apollo was a fraud. Such arguments went along these lines.

You can see Apollo was faked because the space travelers made no such shouts of glee while on the moon, and their photos are strangely devoid of stars.

It is quite clear that the filming took place in a film studio as the lack of spontaneous glee expected in such an environment is palpably obvious.

**Claim 4:** The lunar lander Eagle rested gently on the surface of the Moon in photos, which were taken quite soon after the lunar landing on July 20, 1969.

This causes further problems for those who feel Apollo was not the real deal. The argument goes like this.

It is easily seen that Apollo was a fake as the module rests on soil, which has not been disturbed. On landing, Apollo should have blown up a vast cloud of dust, which would have been obvious in the photos yet it is conspicuously absent.

Obviously a fraud! There is no evidence of the blast, which should be clearly evident.

**Claim 5:** Among the many photos from the Apollo landing are the differentiated indentations of a boot print revealed when Buzz Aldrin raises his leg to take a picture showing the properties of the moon's surface.

A large number of such clear prints were featured in photos taken during the Apollo missions as the space explorers pranced over the moon.

These photos provide another reason for the doubt of some. The thinking is that anyone can see Apollo was a fraud because the space travelers' prints are far too distinct to be made on such a very dry surface.

Prints that very much delineated could only have been made in sand, which was wet. There is definitely no moisture on the Moon so the astronauts must have been filmed somewhere else. Film studio?

**Claim 6:** As Armstrong and Aldrin departed from the lunar surface in July 1969, they left behind parts of the Eagle, a U.S. flag, and some other paraphernalia and tools, including, among other things, a seismometer which they used during their short stay.

Like so many other things the astronauts did this was construed as further evidence of deception.

It is easy to see Apollo was a fake on the grounds that with instruments as powerful as the Hubble Space Telescope, designed for peering into the inaccessible recesses of the Universe researchers should be able to clearly see these artifacts scattered on the surface of the Moon.

Despite this, no such photos have ever been taken. If the Moon landing did take place then there should be plenty of such photos. Where are they?

Why are there no photos? Is it because there is nothing up there to photograph? More evidence of a hoax?

**Claim 7:** A picture taken during the Moon landing shows space explorer Buzz Aldrin on the steps of the Eagle, his bent knees indicating that he is going to move up to the next rung.

This and other pictures are yet another cause of doubt and construed as evidence of a fraud.

The skeptics allege evidence for Apollo being a deception since Aldrin is surrounded by the shadow of the lunar lander, even though he is clearly visible.

Believers in a conspiracy see that many shadows in the Apollo photos as being very interesting and evidence that this photo was not taken on the Moon.

The way they interpret the photo the interplay of shadows could only have occurred with multiple light sources. A situation that could not possibly occur on the Moon.

A situation that is far more likely occurs in a more terrestrial setting such as film studio?

**Claim 8:** When close to the Eagle, Buzz Aldrin was setting up an apparatus for the collection of particles originating from the sun; some strange lights appeared in the photos of him.

The disbelievers see more evidence in this of a hoax as they claim such lights were reflections coming from the lights of the film studio where the Moon landing was faked.

They ask "What are these lights?"

**Claim 9:** If an astronaut wishes to reach the Moon, then the space explorers have to pass through something of great potential danger called the Van Allen radiation belt. This belt goes around the Earth and is definitely very dangerous.

The Apollo missions to the moon were the first ever endeavor of mankind in which living people were transported through the belt.

Conspiracy theorists are sure that the belt would have subjected the astronauts traveling to the Moon to fatal levels of radiation, in spite of the layers of aluminum covering both the inside and outside of the spaceship.

Why weren't the astronauts fried as they passed through the Van Allen belt? There is no Van Allen Belt in a film studio!

**Claim 10:** Many films that were shown of the astronauts on the moon show them bounding in ways that are not earthly.

In order to explain this the skeptics have shown that if you take the film of the landing on the Moon and increase the speed by 250% then the space explorers will appear to be moving in Earth's gravity. The doubters claim that NASA must have used such techniques.

The great leaps of the space travelers are attributed to hidden links and wires some photos are claimed to show these.

The ability to get earthly movement by adjusting a film's speed and the carelessly concealed wires prove a hoax!

**Claim 11:** A prominent photo among the many f photographs from the lunar landings shows a rock with the letter C on it!

The letter seems to be perfectly symmetrical, very unlikely in nature, which usually produces rocks whose markings are rarely of such symmetry.

The skeptics see the stone as a film prop, marked with the C by people associated with the production of the hoax. They say someone carelessly put it in a situation where its revealing nature was visible to all. Someone carelessly kicking it over to reveal a massive deception!

**Claim 12:** Conspiracy theorists assert that acclaimed filmmaker Stanley Kubrick was hired by the US government to film fakes of the first three Moon landings.

There are two main branches of this hypothesis:

(1) This alleges that Kubrick was approached after the 1968 release of his production 2001: A Space Odyssey (released in the year 1968, which was one year before the first lunar landing), after NASA was amazed by the authenticity of the film's space scenes.

(2) Another theory is that Kubrick was approached by NASA to film the lunar landing considerably before this and that the film 2001: A Space Odyssey was a dress rehearsal for what he eventually did.

Is there any proof to back up such extraordinary claims?

In The Shining which was another Kubrick picture, it is claimed that there are some secret messages by Kubrick to the world discreetly informing the world of his part in the fraud.

One of the most revealing is a shirt, worn by a child in a single scene, which says Apollo 11. There are other hints that he is alleged to have subtly insinuated into this film.

In this film, the fact that a room number was 237 was seized on as further evidence of Kubrick's complicity.

The distance from the Earth to the Moon is 238000 miles. Divide that by 1000 then subtract 1 and you have 237!

Finally in 2015 more than 15 years after Stanley Kubrick's passing away in 1999 a video came to light in which Kubrick supposedly concedes that the NASA Moon landings were fraudulent.

T. Patrick Murray, a movie producer, says three days before Kubrick's demise in March 1999 he conversed with Kubrick about this.

In order for this discussion to occur, he had to sign an 88-page Non-Disclosure Agreement to keep the substance of the meeting secret for a long time.

There is a transcript from the meeting of Murray with Kubrick, during which the 2001 Space Odyssey Director confessed on camera that, "All the moon landings were hoaxes, and that I was the individual who filmed them."

As proof or evidence, a recording of the words spoken between Murray and Kubrick has been put on the Internet as well as a video in which an actor pretending to be Kubrick in the interview is shown.

**Claim 13:** One of the photos of an astronaut shows a peculiar object hanging down in a reflection of the astronaut's helmet. Skeptics claim that this reflection indicates a wire or rope suspending a studio light.

There is another intriguing conspiracy which has been disseminated by some. While these people accept the veracity of the Moon landings they see the Moon landings as part of the scheme to impose a World Government by the Illuminati who seek to establish a New World Order.

Much importance is attached to the fact that Buzz Aldrin is supposed to have conducted a Masonic rite on the moon.

This strange belief is mentioned only in passing as the purpose of this book is to present the history of the Apollo project and the claims for and against it being a fraud.

The next chapter will show how these claims are rebuffed by those who have no doubt that the Moon landings were real.

# Evidence Against A Fake

This chapter reproduces each claim against the landing and how it was/is rebutted. It is noteworthy that NASA does not stoop to defend itself against claims of fraud and even murder.

The repudiations of the conspiracy theorists' claims are done by the many millions of people all over the world who are absolutely convinced that the Apollo missions and the Moon landings did occur.

To a man and woman, they see the claims of the conspiracy theorists as a slander on mankind's greatest achievement, often for pecuniary reasons.

**Claim 1:** The flag could not flutter if there were no atmosphere.

**Rebuttal:** There have been many rebuttals of this. Here are three:

(1) The 'fluttering' was the result of vibrations resulting from actions of the astronauts. The lack of an atmosphere accentuated these.

(2) The flag was contained in a slender, cylindrical tube. As it was unfurled it rippled and the small lunar gravity did not damp this as it would on Earth.

(3) The planting of the pole made of aluminum started the pole shaking which caused the flag to wave.

**Claim 2:** Who took the photos of the two astronauts? No one else was supposed to have been on the lunar surface with Armstrong and Aldrin.

**Rebuttal:** There is only one explanation and that is that the cameras were actually mounted on the chests of the astronauts.

All photos taken on the lunar surface by the astronauts were by these cameras or by cameras put on the Moon by the astronauts to take photos.

**Claim 3:** The 'lunar sky' is devoid of stars. Surely this is not so!

**Rebuttal:** For two reasons this claim is easy for defenders of the Moon landing to refute:

(1) The surface of the moon reflects light to such an extent that stars would be difficult to see. For the same reason if the sky is looked at during night in a city very few stars can be seen as the city lights drown out most stars.

On Earth, it is necessary to go to a rural region or a wilderness to see the full panoply of stars.

(ii) Photos taken by the astronauts used very fast exposure settings. Such settings would make it impossible for the stars to be seen.

**Claim 4:** Where is the crater that Eagle should have made? Where is the dust it should have blown as it landed?

**Rebuttal:** The idea that a landing space vehicle will alight with a large jet of fire was at that time in the middle of the twentieth century an invention of the entertainment industry.

When the Eagle landed it did not hover and as it landed it greatly reduced its emission. This is in complete contrast to the landing of the Space X Falcon, which landed on a barge while still emitting a powerful flame in 2017.

**Claim 5:** The very precise boot indentations on the 'lunar surface' would only be possible in wet sand. How can this be possible on a lunar surface completely devoid of water?

**Rebuttal:** Moondust, known more correctly as regolith, is a finely ground powder. Under the microscope, it has a similar appearance as the ash of a volcano.

A foot on this will leave a very exact imprint, which would remain for a long time due to the lack of atmosphere on the Moon.

**Claim 6:** Why it that we haven't any photos of the detritus left by the astronauts on their alleged 'lunar flights' taken by the powerful telescopes now available? Is there nothing to photograph?

**Rebuttal:** Even with our most powerful telescopes, including the Hubble, nothing smaller than a house is visible on the lunar surface.

Further proof of the Moon landing is afforded by photos taken by the unmanned Lunar Reconnaissance Orbiter in 2015, which shows remnants of the earlier flights.

In addition, photographs taken by other countries' satellites have provided proof of the Apollo landings.

**Claim 7:** A photo of Aldrin on the steps from Eagle to the Moon indicates multiple light sources of the types found in film studios! Is this further evidence of a hoax?

**Rebuttal:** Yes there were multiple light sources but they did not come from a film studio. Among these were:

(1) Light from the Sun

(2) Light reflected from Earth

(3) Light reflected from Eagle

(4) Light reflected from the astronauts' suits.

In addition

The surface of the Moon is not flat and as a result, there may be multiple shadows.

**Claim 8:** The strange lights seen in one of the photos of Aldrin were reflections of film studio lights.

When close to the Eagle, Buzz Aldrin was setting up an apparatus for the collection of particles originating from the sun; some strange lights appeared in the photos of him.

The disbelievers see more evidence in this of a hoax as they claim such lights were reflections coming from the lights of the film studio where the Moon landing was faked.

**Rebuttal:** The rebuttals to this are in two forms:

(1) It is implausible to imagine that NASA, if they had faked the Moon landings by spending millions of dollars on films, would make such an error as releasing a photo showing studio lights.

(2) The lights are something called lens flares. Lens flares are an annoying phenomenon caused by what is called light scattering.

The effect is the creation of bright, pentagonal shapes in the photo whose sides depend on characteristics of the camera's lens.

Those familiar with the workings of film studios would know of the problems caused by lens flares!

**Claim 9:** Why weren't the astronauts killed by passage through the Van Allen Belt? Surely if the Apollo landings weren't faked they would have been!

**Rebuttal:** The astronauts were only within the Van Allen Belt for a very short time. This time was not long enough for them to receive more than harmless amounts of radiation.

**Claim 10:** The movements of the astronauts on the moon were as a result of cameras being slowed and the jumps seen were created by hoisting using cables, some of which are visible.

This was very careless on the part of the film studio where the 'missions' were filmed!

**Rebuttal:** The movements of the astronauts on the lunar surface were what would be expected from basic Newtonian mechanics and there were no cranes and cables needed to achieve the very high leaps and bounds seen.

**Claim 11:** It is impossible for a rock with a perfect letter C to occur in nature! Its presence shows that a prop was carelessly left on the floor of the film studio where the Moon landings were filmed!

**Rebuttal:** The letter only appeared in one photo and could be a hair.

Furthermore, there are many rocks on Earth with more amazing shapes on them than the letter C. Shapes which are just as symmetrical.

It is not surprising that a lunar rock might have a C on it.

**Claim 12:** What about Stanley Kubrick's confession?

**Rebuttal:** The family of Stanley Kubrick totally refuted the allegation that he helped make a fraudulent lunar landing film for NASA.

The family says the story that the film producer T Patrick Murray interviewed him on his deathbed where he made a confession that he had helped NASA create a film showing a false Moon landing was a complete untruth.

The announcement of Kubrick's participation in the massive fraud was made just after NASA had claimed to have found the booster rocket of Apollo 16.

By making the claim of a fake film attention would be drawn away from this discovery. If this was the reason for the release of the 'confession' then it was pathetic.

**Claim 13:** One of the photos of an astronaut shows a peculiar object hanging down in a reflection of the astronaut's helmet. Skeptics claim that this reflection indicates a wire or rope suspending a studio light.

What was this mysterious object?

**Rebuttal:** It is a strange fact that no one knows and as it is nearly fifty years ago we will probably never know.

One thing is for certain is that it was not a studio light!

This debate about the veracity of the Moon landings has been going on for a long time.

The defenders of the belief that the landings occurred offer these points as incontrovertible proof that the Apollo program was real.

(1) The USSR, the arch enemy of the USA in the Cold War and the Space Race, did not dispute it.

(2) The vast number of photos, which were taken of a non-terrestrial vista

(3) The 382 kg of rock samples the astronauts brought back. These were not meteorites. No lunar meteorites were found until the 1980s.

The rock samples were identical to those obtained by the Soviet Union through unmanned expeditions.

(4) The huge number of people who worked on the program. This is very significant as Dr. Robert David Grimes of Oxford University has devised an equation which predicts the time that a conspiracy can remain secret.

The equation is based on standard differential equations. It can be made more complicated with adjustments.

An equation emerges that cannot be solved analytically. However approximate solutions can be found using graphical or numerical methods.

From the point of view of the layperson, the results of the deliberations of Dr. Grimes are that the more people who are involved in a conspiracy then the shorter the time that the conspiracy will remain secret.

In the case of the moon landing, hundreds of thousands of people were involved in the Apollo enterprise.

Using the equation of Dr. Grimes we can arrive at the conclusion that if the Apollo program was a vast conspiracy then it would have remained secret for less than four years!

(5) The fact that there were nine Moon missions, not just one. The missions were witnessed by countless thousands in Florida and by millions via TV.

Will we ever know for sure whether the conspiracy theorists are right?

The next chapter will try to answer this question.

# Will We Ever Know For Sure?

In 2009 the Lunar Reconnaissance Orbiter was launched by NASA for unmanned exploration of the moon.

In 2010 NASA flew the Lunar Reconnaissance Orbiter (LRO) near parts of the moon where Apollo 12, 14 and 17 had landed.

One of the objections to the possibility of successful Moon landings was the nonexistence of photographs of the landing sites from powerful telescopes such as the Hubble.

Defenders of the landings had pointed out that photos obtained from any distant camera would not have enough resolution to pick out the remnants of the Apollo missions from the environment in which they lay.

By flying LRO close to the Moon the cameras onboard the space vehicle had enough and sufficient resolution to verify that these missions had indeed taken place and left something behind.

By adjusting the orbit of the LRO the resolution, which permitted the discernment of these remnants was obtained.

The LRO would normally orbit the Moon at an altitude of 31 miles or 52 km however by making these adjustments the LRO flew as low as 13 miles or 22 km.

The LRO still orbits the moon and recently found an Indian spacecraft called Chandrayaan-I which had been lost for eight years.

Doubters of the Apollo landings could well say that as the Lunar Reconnaissance Orbiter was launched by NASA, the photos they have produced of the Moon landings are fakes.

They could claim these photos are just a continuation of the fraud.

They could claim completely correctly that the photos could easily be made with modern computer packages such as

Photoshop.

It used to be said that the camera does not lie. In the hands of a good camera technician equipped with Photoshop, lies are quite possible.

Many are the glamorous film star who has been shocked to see her photo in the gutter press or online kissing someone she does not even know. She is another victim of this skill

What might allay any doubts of the Apollo landing would be photographs taken of any remnants by a completely independent source.

Such evidence is often referred to as third-party evidence. Is there any third-party evidence?

The Selene Luna probe of 2008 which was launched by the Japanese Aerospace Exploration Agency took photos which served to confirm the Apollo landings.

Although the cameras on that mission did not have enough resolution in their cameras to see hardware there were photos of the blown moon dust caused by the landing of Apollo 15.

These photos are exactly like those taken by Apollo 15 itself.

The Indian lunar orbiter Chandrayaan-1, which was rediscovered by the Lunar Reconnaissance Orbiter, one also recorded the same disturbance and photos of it were sent before contact was lost with it.

The Chinese, no fans of the Americans, with their Chang-2 mission in 2010 also reported seeing evidence of the Apollo landings.

Doubters may well say that the Japanese, Indians, and Chinese are in on the conspiracy and hence they will not accept these photographs as evidence at all.

Photographs are not enough! Some physical evidence might allay their doubts.

Will we ever see independent evidence of the Apollo landings assuming they took place? We may yet see the indisputable evidence.

It has been reported a German mission is about to check further whether there is physical evidence of the Apollo Lunar visits.

A group called Part Time scientists (PTS) will send a pair of unmanned rovers to explore the area where Apollo 17 is believed to have landed.

In order to prepare for this mission, PTS has worked with the Audi motor company to devise the rovers.

The reason they are doing this is to compete for the Google Lunar X prize. This is a prize offered by the Google Company for a competition involved in landing vehicles on the Moon.

The flights will take place on a space X rocket. Further mention must be made of space X.

The American visionary and entrepreneur Elon Musk founded SpaceX in 2002. It has successfully developed the Falcon rocket and the Dragon spacecraft.

It has lofty goals including a return to the Moon and the colonization of Mars. More will be said on this in a later chapter.

Once on the Moon the German rover will go to where Apollo 17 landed. It will also carry out some scientific tests.

Apollo 17 is of particular interest to some conspiracy theorists that believe that the lunar landings did take place but Apollo 17 was the last as it involved a meeting with alien beings who were not from the planet Earth.

This belief is of course in contrast to the majority of conspiracy theorists who believe that no Apollo landings were ever carried out or the fringe group who believe that the landings were part of the plot by the Illuminati to establish a New World Order!

We won't dwell on this as the Illuminati seem to everywhere from pop concerts to the Moon. They have been blamed for everything from the rises of Hitler and Communism to the death of Michael Jackson!

In the next chapter, we will look at the future of space travel and developments that may well see trips to the Moon become possible for those who wish to go there and are wealthy enough to do so.

When and if such travel becomes commonplace then if there are still, or ever were, Apollo landing sites then it is certain that visits to these sites will be high on the list of places for lunar tourists to visit.

At the present time, NASA is not keen for others to go to the sites where the Apollo landings were. This negativity has further inflamed the suspicions of those who suspect cover-ups and frauds.

It is unfortunate that NASA is adopting this

posture as it attracts suspicion. Perhaps the reason for the wish that others do not go to the sites is that they desire to make scientific measurements there and see how much has changed in 50 years.

They need a site, which is undisturbed.

Those with suspicion about their motives will say their purpose is to plant material there. The purpose being to make people believe the Apollo missions occurred.

Even if lunar tourism does not become a reality there may be other reasons for mankind to return to the Moon. It is to be hoped that these reasons are not military.

Space is supposed to be demilitarized.

Treaties were signed during the Cold War to prohibit the militarization of space.

There was an Outer Space Treaty in 1967 and a Moon Treaty in 1979. Unfortunately now with the extreme economic importance of satellites, the disappearance of the Soviet bloc and the rise of cyber espionage and crime completely new circumstances exist.

The rise of the militarization of space is quite possible.

Even if there is no human return to the Moon for military reasons there may well be commercial ones.

What about the commercial exploitation of the moon? There are a number of learned people such as Professor Ian Crawford of London speculating on possible riches in the lunar soil.

One of the holy grails for the energy of the future is fusion and one method of achieving fusion is an isotope of helium called helium-3.

This is believed to be abundant on the Moon. It is also believed that the lunar surface, so often the recipient of hits by meteors, will be a source of platinum group elements, which are very valuable.

No matter what the reason it is almost certain, barring catastrophe, that human beings will visit the Moon in the future and when they do so the question of whether the

Apollo Landings occurred should be forever answered.

The Moon landings will never be verified for some. No matter what is done their position will always be one of disbelief.

Such people can be compared to the believers in a flat Earth; a Universe aged only a few thousand years or a Sun that goes around the Earth.

However, most people who have beliefs one way or the other will have those beliefs confirmed or discredited in the future.

# Future of Space Travel

**Satellites:** these played a major role in the Space Race from its start until its conclusion in 1969. The space race really began on October 4, 1957, when the Russians, or Soviets as they were then usually known, launched Sputnik 1.

Sputnik 1 was the first orbiting object that had ever been launched by human beings.

Sputnik 1 moved in an elliptical path around the earth. It only weighed 83.6 kg or 183.9 pounds and only had a radius of about 30 cm or a foot.

Its only function was to broadcast beeping noises. One orbit of the Earth took about 98 minutes.

Since that time about 8000 satellites have been put into orbits of varying types and heights and for a huge variety of reasons.

Some move in an orbit that is called a geostationary orbit, which means they move in such a way that they are always above the same place on Earth.

Most of the 8000 satellites are no longer in orbit and have disintegrated or fallen to the earth. Of the 8000 there are about 3000 still in the heavens.

On a clear night, it is possible to see evidence of them. They appear as silently moving stars. Most of these satellites are not operational.

In other words, they do nothing except constitute what has been called space junk.

About 900 are still working, with about half of those still working coming from the USA.

Since the tiny beginnings of Sputnik 1, the size and weight of satellites have greatly increased.

Terrestar-1, which was launched in 2009, has wings of a length of about 32 m or 106 feet. It is a communications satellite.

No less than 58 countries have satellites, although they usually were taken into orbit by the rockets of other countries.

Only 10 countries have actually launched satellites, although there is a consortium of European countries that have used Arianne rockets in order to launch them.

**Are any trips to the moon or the planets planned?** If you Google along these lines you will encounter nothing more than speculation with estimates of decades before this may occur.

Rocketry has now become the province of private enterprise with a very large number of companies throughout the world getting involved in this field.

When private enterprise gets involved in anything then things often happen, particularly if there is money to be made.

There is talk of paid travel around the moon with tickets costing millions and millions of dollars. Prominent in this group of space entrepreneurs is Sir Richard Branson, founder of the Virgin Group of companies.

Company was mentioned.

SpaceX is an American company founded in 2002 by Elon Musk. Its achievements include the Falcon rocket, which successfully landed in 2017 on a barge after launching and the Dragon spacecraft.

Among its future goals are a return to the Moon and eventually the colonization of Mars.

In the last years of his rule, President Obama made predictions of trips to Mars during the 2030s. He mused about a collaborative effort with the Russians.

With a new president who seems to have an unusually positive view of the Russians for a US President, this may possibly occur.

Some of the private organizations mentioned before have talked of one-way trips to the Red Planet resulting in the establishment of colonies there.

Presumably once there they would build

spaceships with which to return to Earth.

A survey found that there were two hundred thousand people who would be happy to participate in a one-way trip to Mars. The urge to explore and venture to places unvisited is alive and well in humanity.

The desire to be part of a great adventure, something bigger than any individual, is very much a part of many, if not most, people.

**How Long Does It Take To Travel To Mars?** It takes about 150 to 300 days in order to travel from Earth to the red planet Mars.

This variability results from factors such as the launch speeds of the rocket, the alignment of the two planets, and the length of the trip needed in order to traverse the vast distance separating earth from Mars.

**How fast do we need to go in order to travel in space?** There are certain speeds, which have to be attained in order to do certain things in space.

These are called cosmic velocities. The first cosmic velocity is the speed needed in order to get into orbit around the earth. This is 7.9 km/s.

The second cosmic velocity is a much greater speed. This is the speed required to break free of the Earth's gravitational field. It is 11.2 km/s.

The next and third cosmic velocity is that required to break free from the gravitational pull of the solar system. This is about 42 km/s.

The final or fourth cosmic velocity is the speed which must be attained if you wish to leave the Milky Way.

This is a huge speed. It is 320 km/s or 192 miles a second.

**How fast can rockets go?** So far we have made rockets, which can propel objects to the furthest reaches of the solar system.

Rockets are capable of great speeds but in order to reach them, they have to carry ever-increasing amounts of fuel.

This is a massive problem, which puts limits on the possible speed, which can be reached by a rocket using our existing technologies.

The largest possible speed for a rocket has been estimated at about 36,000 mph or 16.7 km/s.

**Will rockets take us to deep space?** It would seem that if we consider the previous sections on cosmic velocities and the maximum possible velocities of rockets then using our current technologies to travel beyond outside the Solar System is impossible.

A completely different technology or approach will be needed.

Before we consider travel beyond the Solar System it would probably be best to achieve travel to the other parts of the Solar System.

The decisions necessary to get the vast sums of money in order to carry this out may be deferred so that attention and resources can be brought on major problems on our own planet such as renewable energy and global warming.

The previous program to land someone on the Moon was as we have seen a child of the Cold War. It is doubtful that there would have been a Space Race without the spur of that.

**The Distances between Stars and the speed of light:** The distance between stars is measured in light-years. A light-year is the distance light travels in one year.

Light travels at 300,000 kilometers per second (186,000 miles per second). Space is so vast that you would need to travel about 100000 light-years to cross our galaxy, the Milky Way.

Earth is about 30000 light-years from the center of the Milky Way.

The speed of light is a natural limit to speed according to Einstein's Theory of Relativity.

Traveling at the speed of light is impossible but it is theoretically possible to travel near the speed of light.

If you do so though some strange things happen. If you were traveling for one year near the speed of light when you returned to Earth you would find that thousands of years would have passed while you were away.

Despite this frightening fact it is clear that if we really wish to travel beyond our solar system travel close to the speed of light will be essential.

**Is any research being done to make a vehicle which could travel at speeds near that of light?** If interstellar travel is carried out it will not be in rockets. They will never be able to take us to the stars!

It is possible, in the laboratory, for particles to be accelerated to speeds near that of light but so far our spacecraft have not even come close.

Many ideas are being trialed though. One could see a Mars trip in three days rather than the 150 minimum using rockets.

The momentum of light photons would provide the thrust. The photons would come from huge lasers stationed on Earth and they would beat against sails on the space vehicle.

Although this sounds odd it has actually been done on a small scale but needs scaling up.

Yet another weird sounding idea is the impossible EM Drive. It shouldn't work but does. Scientists are playing with it.

It seems to completely contradict Newton's Third Law however it works. It will be interesting to see if anything comes of this.

No less an authority than Stephen Hawking, brilliant and world famous British mathematician has stated that a mission to Alpha Centauri, the nearest star of the solar system, is possible within a generation.

He has joined forces with NASA to pursue this lofty scheme. His clarion call to us is a summons for this great leap into the cosmos and a reminder that it is our nature to fly.

The name given to the spaceship he and NASA envisage for interstellar travel is the nano-starship. As currently seen it could travel at one-fifth the speed of light.

One possible propulsion system involves what are known as Lorentz forces.

The person responsible for this extraordinary idea is an American professor from Cornell University called Mason Peck. He has received a grant to investigate this.

**Wormholes?** As we have seen movement near the speed of life through the immensity of space completely alters what we would expect as regards time. A possible method of traveling through time and space is using things called wormholes.

If the theory is right, we would have a means of enormously reducing vast journeys involving enormous lengths of time across the universe to practicable times.

Wormholes are predicted by Einstein's general relativity theory. Presuming they actually exist then their possible use is fraught with danger.

Einstein himself, as early 1935, postulated passages through space-time by the use of wormholes. A wormhole has two spheroidally shaped mouths, joined by a throat.

Their existence has been mathematically predicted however their discovery has not yet occurred. A means of locating them would be the unusual behavior of light as a result of gravity in the neighborhood of a wormhole.

Traveling through one would not be as simple as entering a channel. Wormholes are predicted to be incredibly small and very unstable. The illustrious British scientist Stephen Hawking has discounted their possible use.

Interstellar travel is said to be a generation away. Perhaps travel to the furthest stars may be possible but at the moment apart from suggestions to use wormholes how this could be possible has not been theorized.

Perhaps we need to concentrate on manned flight to the planets of our solar system and in a generation turn attention to traveling to the nearest stars.

Once that is done we may know enough to travel to the ends, if they exist, of the universe.

# Summary

Conspiracy theories arise in many ways and forms. Modern technology combined with human nature mean that such theories arise more quickly than in the past.

The principal focus of this book has been on the conspiracy theories, which arose as a result of the American Moon landings in the late 1960s and early 1970s.

These conspiracy theories can be divided into two categories:

(1) Those which accept the veracity of the Moon landings but associate all sorts of cover-ups such as involvement of the Illuminati or contact with aliens.

(2) A belief held by a much greater number of people that the Moon landings never took place.

It is to the last conspiracy theory that most attention has been given.

The Moon landing must be viewed through the prism of the Cold War. That strange conflict dominated the world for more than four decades.

The Moon landings are unlikely to have occurred without the Cold War.

The feeling of success that the Americans enjoyed as a result of these landings, whether real or not, helped to affirm the success in their minds of their way of doing things and of their social system.

The Moon landings were viewed by countless millions of people who were given the unmistakable message that America had superior technology in comparison to that of the Russians.

The Moon landings were part of the Space Race. A race, which began in 1957 when the Russians launched Sputnik 1.

The rockets and technology for these landings had their origin in the V2 rockets of the Nazis in World War II.

This technology was being developed by both the Americans and Russians, predominantly for military purposes in order to carry nuclear warheads that would devastate the cities of the other side in the Cold War.

The rockets used in the Space Race were developed from rockets which had military purposes.

In America, a succession of rockets was developed under the leadership of Wernher von Braun from Germany. He was put in charge of the program whose aim was to put a man on the Moon in less than a decade.

Huge rockets called Saturns were developed for this purpose. They were carefully tested and in the late 1960s were ready for primetime.

A series of tests were administered where every facet of the final Moon landing was tested. On July 20, 1969, two American astronauts descended to the lunar surface and won for America the Space Race.

Shortly after the Apollo program finished in 1972 claims started to emerge that the Moon landings were fake.

Evidence for this fake was seen in flags that flapped nonexistent stars, shadows which were all wrong and many other possible reasons, which were advanced.

It was claimed that Stanley Kubrick, the famous filmmaker, had confessed in a mysterious video when he was near death that he had been hired by NASA in order to make a film of the Moon landings.

As already mentioned some other conspiracy theories did accept that the Moon landings were real but saw the involvement of a shadowy group called the Illuminati.

Others saw aliens concerned about human invasion of their domain.

Each of these 'pieces of evidence of conspiracy' has been debunked. Often the debunking has been done, not officially, but by the many millions of people who revere the astronauts.

They see the successful achievement of the program to land them on the Moon as an expression of what humanity is capable of when it turns its efforts to something worthwhile, instead of cruelty and destruction.

NASA has provided photographs of Apollo landing remnants, as have others.

A trip by Germans to an Apollo site is planned. The controversy as to whether the Moon landings actually occurred will probably never be solved until man returns to the Moon.

Will mankind ever return to space? There are plans for commercial flights to the Moon.

There have been suggestions of a trip to Mars in the 2030s.

Travel into deep space beyond the solar system is impossible using modern technology. The technology that might make such travel possible is still being developed.

Even if it existed travel to the furthest reaches of the Milky Way would still be impossible. Or is it?

Wormholes, postulated by Einstein, may provide a solution to the problem of reaching these distant places.

Such a distinguished scientist as Stephen Hawking thinks that this is not possible but given the extraordinary ingenuity of the human race, some way of doing this will probably be found.

# Conclusion

Space and Space Travel are huge and fascinating subjects.

In the years 1946-1972 they were an ever present part of human life.

Since then there have been many unmanned missions into space but no manned flight except in orbit around the Earth.

Things seem to be different now. We may return to the Moon. There is talk of travel to Mars in a few decades. Travel to other stars within a generation.

We are at the brink of a new age of discovery.

It is to be hoped that the resources to enable this discovery will be found. It is vital for the survival of our species that we stop fighting, stop doubting and resume exploring!

Good Luck and God bless.

# 911 CONSPIRACY

What Really Happened:

9/11 and the War On Terror

Phil Coleman

# Introduction

To say the events of September 11, 2001, changed the world is an understatement. The global impact of the attacks that occurred in New York City, Washington DC, and Shanksville, Pennsylvania could never be measured.

Out of the attacks came drastically increased security world-wide, rampant xenophobia, a war that might possibly never end, and forever damaged relations between the United States and the Middle East.

In times of crisis and attacks such as these, people tend to look for answers as to why such events happened. In the case of 9/11, this led to rampant conspiracy theories about

the attacks that even close to twenty years
later still prevail.

# The Day of the Attacks

The morning of Tuesday, September 11, 2001, started out as a normal day until it wasn't. The coordinated terrorist attacks of that day seemed unbelievable even as they were happening as there had not been a foreign attack on American soil since the attack on Pearl Harbor on December 7, 1941, which launched the United States into World War II. On the fateful day of September 11, 2001, history repeated itself.

The coordinated attacks against the United States were a result of nineteen Al-Qaeda terrorists hijacking four different commercial flights from carriers United Airlines and American Airlines.

The first plane, American Airlines Flight 11, hit the North Tower of The World Trade Center at 8:46 a.m. It departed from Logan International Airport in Boston and was heading to Los Angeles.

At first, the plan colliding with the skyscraper was thought to be an accident as an incident such as that was not far-fetched. In 1945, a United States military plane struck the Empire State Building. However, the following attacks proved it was anything but.

News crews were soon on the scene reporting the crash while witnesses and those watching around the world wondered and waited for answers.

In the short time frame between the first and second attacks on the World Trade Center, much speculation was going on among New Yorkers as to what was actually happening.

This is where many of the still prevalent conspiracy theories originated. One of the most common being that the plans were in fact missiles launched by either the terrorists on the planes or by the United States Military attacking its own people to get into another war.

Those who did not see the plane crash but saw the aftermath thought it was a fire. Paper flying from the windows (The World Trade Center housed many offices and at the time digit file storage was not as it is today) caused witnesses to think it was a parade of some sort.

A firefighter with the New York City Fire Department later stated that the vast amount of paper in the towers led to the fires burning extremely hot, as the chemicals in paper are known to be very flammable and cause fast, burning and hotter than average fires.

The firefighter estimated that had the attacks taken place today with less paper being used in offices, the fire would not have been as hot and more lives could have been saved. The mass amount of jet fuel also was a catalyst in the extremely hot and fast-burning fires. All of the planes were set to travel across the country to California.

About only twenty minutes later United Airlines Flight 175 which also departed from Logan Airport hit the South Tower of The World Trade Center at 9:03 a.m.

The second plane hitting the South Tower proved this was not an accident and as the world would soon learn, it was an act of terrorism.

The third plane, American Airlines Flight 77 from Dulles International Airport in Washington, DC crashed into the Pentagon in Arlington, Virginia at 9:37 a.m.

The final hijacked plane, United Airlines Flight 93 crashed in Somerset County, Pennsylvania. It departed from Newark Airport in New Jersey and was bound for

San Francisco. The intended target for the plan was supposed to be the Capitol Building in Washington, DC

It was also believed but never confirmed The White House was also a potential target for this flight. In 2002, Khalid Sheikh Mohammed and Ramzi bin al-Shibh, who are suspected for helping mastermind the attacks, confirmed the target was only the Capitol.

Passengers on Flight 93 had received phone calls warning them about the attacks and plane hijackings. Once the flight was taken over, pilots de-activated the auto-pilot controls to hinder the hijacker's plans. However, one of the hijackers, Ziad Jarrah was trained as a pilot and was able to fly the plane back towards Washington, DC

Soon after the hijackers took over the plane, the passengers voted to take it back from them. Cabin recordings and recorded phone calls confirmed the passengers' takeover of the plane.

During the takeover, the plane crashed in Pennsylvania at 10:00 a.m. All 44 passengers, crew, and hijackers were killed in the crash. No one on the ground was killed in the crash. Upon learning about the intended target and re-directed plane, Vice President Dick Cheney said, "I think an act of heroism just took place on that plane."

At 9:42 a.m. the Federal Aviation Administration (FAA) grounded all civilian and commercial flights in the United States. Flights already in the air were told to land immediately. All United States international flights were either told to turn back or were directed to land in Mexico or Canada.

International flights planned enroute for the United States were canceled for three days. A total of 500 planes turned around. This led to thousands of passengers being stranded across the world. Canada received 226 of these flights.

This order caused mass confusion for airports, air traffic controllers, news outlets, and impending passengers. During this uncertain time, there were many false and contradicting reports. One of these reports was that a car bomb had detonated at the US State Department Headquarters in Washington. Another flight was suspected of having been hijacked, Delta Air Lines Flight 1989. Pilots confirmed the report false and landed in Cleveland, Ohio.

Miscommunication on the day of the attacks was also a problem. At 8:32 a.m. the FAA was notified that Flight 11 had been hijacked. They notified the North American Aerospace Defense Command (NORAD), which launched two F-15 planes from a National Guard Base in Massachusetts to try to intercept the commercial flight.

Due to miscommunication and slow communication, NORAD only had 9 minutes notice about Flight 11. No other notices were given to them about the other hijacked flights.

After the Twin Towers had been hit, more fighter jets were assembled from Langley Air Force Base in Virginia. At 10:20 a.m. after the crashes, Dick Cheney issued an order for any civilian plane that was identified as being hijacked to be shot down by the military.

These orders were not relayed and no action was taken on part of the fighter jets. It is possible had these ordered been properly communicated and received, the loss of life due to the attacks might have been less.

Throughout the day, President George W. Bush was flown around to various locations for safety measures. Many criticized this even though it was imperative to keep the President safe during a domestic terror attack.

President Bush not being readily available on 9/11 allowed for Dick Cheney to take over the role. This caused some controversy in the United States considering Cheney was extremely unpopular.

During all four hijackings, passenger's cellphone records and witness testimony provided details on the hijackers and the exact horrific events that took place aboard the plans. Descriptions and details about the hijackers themselves were also reported by the passengers who helped in the later investigation of the attacks.

Passengers reported the hijackers used mace, tear gas, box cutter knives, and pepper spray to gain control of the pilots and flight attendants. It was also reported several people aboard the planes had been stabbed.

It was also estimated the hijackers had killed pilots, flight attendants, and several random passengers. Reports from Flights 11, 175, and 93 stated that the hijackers had bombs. During the 9/11 Commission investigation, the FBI found no traces of explosives at the crash sites. Reports from the Commission state that any bombs seen aboard the plane were most likely fake.

In our constantly connected world, it is hard to believe or remember a time when we couldn't get instant news alerts and know exactly what was happening during a major crisis such as 9/11. That was the reality of the day and led to mass and justified fear and wonder.

Within less than two hours, The United States had experienced four different terrorist attacks. Both of the Twin Towers completely collapsed in only an hour and 42 minutes after the planes crashed into them.

In total, the attacks killed 2,996 people, injured over 6,000, and caused almost $10 billion in infrastructure and property damage. The attacks were also the single deadliest event in American history for firefighters and law enforcement officials, killing a total of 343 firefighters and 72 police officers. The Army and Navy both lost personnel in the attacks.

265 passengers and crew aboard all four planes died. There were no survivors on any of the hijacked planes. A total of 90 countries lost citizens in the attacks. The states of New York followed by New Jersey lost the most citizens, with the city of Hoboken, New Jersey having lost the most citizens.

The 9/11 attacks are still the deadliest terror attacks in world history. Although hundreds of law enforcement, firefighters, and military members were killed in the attacks, the vast majority of those killed were civilians.

It was estimated about 14,154 people were typically in both Twin Towers every weekday by 8:45 a.m. On September 11, 2001, an estimate of over 17,000 were said to have been in the Towers that day.

Many in the towers who were below the area of impact were able to escape. Those at the higher floors above the impact area were not able to evacuate.

In the weeks after the attacks, the death toll was estimated to be over 6,000, which was well over the amount eventually confirmed. The New York City Medical Examiner was only able to identify about 1,600 causalities based on DNA and other evidence. Over 10,000 bone fragments and tissue samples were collected by the Medical Examiner and have not been matched.

In 2006, bone fragments were still being found by construction workers repairing a bank near where the Twin Towers once stood. After the attacks, the then-closed Fresh Kills Landfill in Staten Island was re-opened and used for debris collection to find any human remains.

In 2010, the landfill was searched again. Archeologists found 72 more sets of human remains. These remains were matched to some of the DNA on file and led to several missing being identified as having been killed in the attacks.

On March 20, 2015, another victim was identified. This brought the death toll to 1,640. Since then, there are a remaining 1,113 victims who have not been identified.

# Planning The Attacks

The day of the attacks, The United States government immediately suspected the Taliban and Al-Qaeda, both politically motivated Islamic extremist terrorist groups.

Osama bin Laden, the leader and founder of the Al-Qaeda group orchestrated the 9/11 attacks. Bin Laden was born into a family of Saudi Arabian billionaires. He dropped out of college to fight against the Soviet Union invasion of Afghanistan.

Bin Laden formed Al-Qaeda in 1988 and soon was responsible for many acts of terrorism throughout the world including the 1998 bombings of two United States Embassies in Tanzania and Nairobi, Kenya.

Bin Laden was on the FBI's list of Ten Most Wanted Fugitives as well as the Most Wanted Terrorists. From 2001 to 2011 (prior to his death at the hands of the United States Navy SEALS), the FBI placed a $25 million bounty for his capture.

A CIA analyst, Michael Scheuer, who spearheaded the CIA's mission to find Bin Laden, said he was "motivated by a belief that US foreign policy has oppressed, killed, or otherwise harmed Muslims in the Middle East."

Scheuer also stated bin Laden condemned the United States for its secular government. He called for Americans to convert to Islam and "reject the immoral acts of fornication, homosexuality, intoxicants, gambling, and usury."

Several days after the attacks, bin Laden declared, neither he nor his group was responsible. In the months before the 2004 American presidential election, bin Laden confessed he had organized and carried out the attacks.

In 2006, a video showed bin Laden discussing and planning the attacks with two of the hijackers, Hamza al-Ghamdi and Wail al-Shehri. The United States never officially indicated bin Laden in the attacks, he was a suspect from the beginning.

Bin Laden stated in 2004 he came up with the plan to attack the World Trade Center in

1982. Al-Qaeda member, Khalid Sheikh Mohammed helped planned the logistics of the attacks. Mohammed was arrested in 2003 and is currently being held at Guantánamo Bay. He admitted his involvement with 9/11 as well as involvement in the 1993 World Trade Center bombings, also planned by Al-Qaeda.

He was inspired by the high-rise buildings in Israel being caused by American influence in the Middle East. While there were many motivations for the attacks, the primary was Bin Laden's hope to "destroy and bankrupt the United States."

Frustrations with President George W. Bush as well as the United States' growing influence over the Middle East culturally, and the influx of American troops in the Middle East and Northern Africa were said to be secondary motives.

The root and planning of the attacks were orchestrated and planned several years before they occurred. In 1998, the director of the C.I.A warned then-president Bill Clinton that Al-Qaeda had plans to attack the United States as well as the training airplane hijacking. Based on bin Laden and Al-Qaeda's history, it was only a matter time before they struck in the United States.

FBI agents working on counterterrorism task forces received recordings from the NSA in 1999 of the alleged hijackers discussing plans to attack the United States.

It was also reported the FBI had Intel that the hijacker, Khalid al-Mihdhar had planned to come to the United States prior to the attack. The FBI urged the CIA to put Khalid al-Mihdhar on the watch list. However, due to internal conflicts, this did not happen.

Senior C.I.A analyst, Richard Clarke said in June 2001, "convinced that a major series of attacks was about to come." Officials believed the attacks would take place in either Iraq or Saudi Arabia.

Other F.B.I and C.I.A at various field offices around the country received Intel about potential attacks several months before they happened. An F.B.I agent in Phoenix alerted the F.B.I headquarters office as well as the New York field office that, "the possibility of a coordinated effort by Osama bin Laden to send students to the United States to attend civil aviation universities and colleges."

The same agent suggested an investigation of all students of Middle Eastern descent in all flight schools in the United States. Only one known individual enrolled in a flight school was reported to the F.B.I and questioned.

French citizen, Zacarias Moussaoui who was enrolled in a Minnesota flight school was reported for asking "suspicious questions." Moussaoui was arrested by the FINS and charged with conspiracy as he admitted his involvement in Al-Qaeda and helping plan the 9/11 attacks.

In July of 2001, Jordan intelligence officials obtained information stating Al-Qaeda was planning an attack against the United States involving airplanes, and that the code name for the attack was "Big Wedding."

On August 6, 2001, the President's daily briefing memo from the C.I.A, warned that Osama bin Laden was determined to strike in the United States.

The baffling lack of communication between government law enforcement agencies was due to a Justice Department policy implemented in 1995 that limited intelligence sharing. This policy was followed in part by the DCIA and N.S.A not wanting to admit to utilizing "sensitive sources and methods" for obtaining information such as tapped phones and potentially using unorthodox methods.

In either late 1998 or early 1999, bin Laden organized for four people to obtain Saudi Arabian visas which would allow them easy entrance to the United States.

Two of these individuals were from Yemen and could not as easily get into the United States. Instead, they were taken to Asia to obtain visas.

Four of the hijackers, Mohamed Atta, Marwan al-Shehhi, Ziad Jarrah, and Ramzi bin al-Shibh, were all living in Hamburg, Germany prior to the attacks in what was known was the Al-Qaeda Hamburg Cell. Two other Al-Qaeda members, one a part of the Hamburg Cell and one found in Spain are currently in prison for their involvement in planning the attacks.

A total of 19 individuals were selected by bin Laden to carry out the attacks. Fifteen were from Saudi Arabia, and the rest were from Egypt, the United Arab Emirates, and Lebanon.

The day of the attacks, they were grouped into four teams with one in each group trained as a pilot and either three or four who were trained to take over the planes, these individuals were referred to as the "muscle hijackers."

The first of the eventual hijackers to arrive in the United States were Khalid al-Mihdhar and Nawaf al-Hazmi. They moved to San Diego in January 2000. Another pilot, Hani Hanjour moved to San Diego in December 2000, where he trained at a local flight school.

The other three hijacker pilots, Mohamed Atta, Marwan al-Shehhi, and Ziad Jarrah, were trained by a flight school in Florida where they reportedly only were interested in learning how to land planes and not take off. Both flight schools came under much scrutiny and criticism after their history with training the hijackers became public.

Despite the lack of cooperation between federal law enforcement agencies prior to the attacks, afterwards they were able to identify all the hijackers and trace them back to

Osama bin Laden and Al-Qaeda within seventy-two hours.

Identifying the hijackers was such a speedy process because none of them disguised their names or used falsified travel documents. A bystander to the World Trade Center attacks found a passport on the ground belonging to Satam al-Suqam and handed it to N.Y.P.D officer on the scene.

Before officials knew of the involvement of Osama bin Laden and Al-Qeada, Iraqi terrorists were suspected to be the culprits behind the attacks as Iraqi dictator Saddam Hussein was known to support terrorist groups and had ties to the Taliban.

At first, bin Laden denied he had any involvement with the attacks. He was quoted as saying on September 18, 2001, "I stress that I have not carried out this act, which appears to have been carried out by individuals with their own motivation."

Despite his denial, government officials knew he was involved and took action. In 2004, bin Laden finally officially admitted to the attacks.

# The Aftermath

After the attacks, the American people were immediately impacted. Many police and rescue workers from all over the country traveled to New York to help with the efforts. Blood donations increased exponentially. Relief funds were set up around the country to help victims' families as over 3,000 children lost a parent in the attacks.

Several companies that were located in the World Trade Center lost over half of their employees. Several other buildings were damaged in the attacks including St. Nicholas Greek Orthodox Church, a Marriott Hotel, and two buildings of the World

Financial Center. Only one section of the Pentagon was completely destroyed.

Contingency programs were set up for government workers and facilities in case of another attack. Homeland Security Act of 2002 as well as the Patriot Act was passed as a direct result of the attacks.

The Patriot Act was controversial and caused much debate around the country. The law passed in October 2001 increases government and law enforcement power to investigate potential terrorists and terrorist activities.

It allowed for increased border security and increased criminal punishments for terrorists. The law also defined several acts of terrorism punishable by the government including, attacking a mass transit system, using a biological weapon, supporting terrorism and computer hacking.

The Patriot Act provides provisions for financial compensation for victims of terrorism and their families.

The National Security Agency (NSA) also had their power and duties expanded as a result of the attacks. The agency was given the right of conducting warrantless surveillance on various communications. This was highly criticized as it allowed the NSA eavesdrop on citizens and people overseas without a warrant or even just cause.

Since the 9/11 attacks, the NSA's power and duties have exponentially increased. The NSA's duties have been vital in fighting the War on Terror. With constantly new and emerging technology being utilized for terror and related criminal acts, the NSA must stay ahead of these trends to combat worldwide and domestic terrorists.

The increased power granted to the NSA has caused much controversy and received criticism from citizens of the United States and the world. The right to eavesdrop and obtain information without a warrant is considered a violation of rights by many, even when the information is used to combat terrorism.

In 2013, NSA contractor, Edward Snowden famously leaked documents stating the NSA was operating worldwide.

Another Congressional Act that was passed as a direct result of 9/11 was the Authorization for Use of Military Force against Terrorists. Passed on September 14, 2001, the act, still in effect today allows for the President to use "necessary and appropriate force" against anyone who "planned, authorized, committed or aided" to the 9/11 attacks. It also allowed anyone who harbored these individuals to be punished as well.

After the attacks, numerous countries condemned the attacks and showed support for the United States. Many Islamic countries did not show their support for the United States which led to strained relations and an increase of hate crimes against Muslims in America and the rest for the world.

There were reports of celebrations after the attacks in Palestine and Jordan. Iraqi government officials publicly condemned the attacks, but privately many high-ranking Iraqis were supported the causes of Osama Bin Laden.

Muslim Americans also condemned the attacks. Many American-based Muslim groups called "upon Muslim Americans to come forward with their skills and resources to help alleviate the sufferings of the affected people and their families."

At this time, the increase of hate crimes against Muslim Americans increased exponentially. President Bush visited the largest Muslim center in Washington, DC and called for all Muslim's to be "treated with respect." Attacks of mosques and one murder of a man suspected to be a Muslim in Mesa, Arizona. Individuals of South Asian decent were also targeted as one of the hijackers was Lebanese.

A study later conducted state during the days after the attacks; people presumed to be of Middle Eastern descent were more likely to be victims of hate crimes. They study concluded that between September 11-17, 2001 there were a total of 645 hate crimes committed against those presumed to be Middle Eastern or South Asian. Crimes such as vandalism, shooting, harassment, arson, and assault were reported.

The economies of the United States as well as many other countries suffered in the weeks after the attacks. The New York Stock Exchange was closed from September 11-17 and reopened to decade lows.

In New York City, an estimated $2.8 billion were lost in wages in the three months after the attacks. The United States government provided $11.2 billion to the New York City Government in September 2001 and another $10.2 billion in 2002.

The cultural impact of the 9/11 attacks is one of the most profound yet overlooked aspects of the aftermath of 9/11. After the attacks, patriotism in the United States became much more prominent than before. An increase of family-friendly activities and an emphasis on spending time with family emerged.

Church attendance soared in the months following the attacks. Certain songs were removed from the radio due to having questionable lyrics and messages. Many television shows, books, and movies toned down violent content.

This aspect of American society has remained in full force since the weeks after 9/11 and has created a rampant culture of people, creative works, and news outlets being politically correct, or P.C. Despite an increase of xenophobia, many creative projects have been criticized by the public for racial insensitivity as well as other themes.

These thematic elements were a reflection of society trying to find answers as to why such a tragic event happened. An emphasis on family, togetherness, patriotism, and other actives and emotions deemed positive were a coping mechanism.

Increased security at airports, public events, and the daily terror alert soon implemented after 9/11 led to an increase in paranoia and anxiety. This paranoia and anxiety, as well as a search for answers and the truth, led to an uprising of conspiracy theories.

Health issues besides depression, anxiety, and paranoia were brought on by the toxic fumes from the buildings, airplane parts, and jet fuel has been a major impact on those present during the attacks. More than 2,500 known contaminates and carcinogens were spread across New York City when the Towers collapsed.

The toxins present in the buildings and planes have led to an estimated 18,000 people having developed some sort of illness. Several people have died due to complications from the exposure and have been included in the 9/11 Memorial in New York City.

After the attacks, the Bush Administration ordered the Environmental Protection Agency (EPA) to issue warnings about the air quality in New York City. Upon investigation, the EPA concluded the air quality returned to normal in June 2002.

These toxins have caused illnesses in many people of all ages who lived in Lower Manhattan and Chinatown during the time of the attacks. An environmental health center has been conducting studies on children whose mothers were pregnant on 9/11 and who were exposed to the toxic fumes.

The rescue workers from the NYPD, FDNY, and other agencies have also reported numerous lung diseases since the attacks. A study published in April 2010, reported 30-40% of rescue workers who reported lung illnesses showed little or no improvement following treatment. Many reported symptoms started within the first year after working the attack scene.

The numerous individuals suffering from health problems brought on by the attacks led to several legal issues citing who should be responsible for paying the healthcare costs. In October 2006, a federal judge rejected New York City's refusal to pay for healthcare costs of the city's rescue workers. This led to many suits against the city.

Government officials also urged people to continue living and working near the site of the attacks, despite warnings the area was safe. This led to officials including the head of the EPA and then-Mayor Rudi Giuliani receiving much criticism for their irresponsible actions.

On December 2, 2010, Congress passed the James L. Zadroga 9/11 Health and Compensation Act. The Act set up a $4.2 billion fund to create the World Trade Center Health Program, which provides treatment for long-term illnesses as a result of the 9/11 attacks. President Barack Obama signed the bill into law on January 2, 2011.

Not only did the 9/11 attacks impact the policies and laws of the United States, other countries enacted new policies to combat terrorism. Canada passed the first anti-terrorism law in the country's history The United Kingdom and New Zealand also passed anti-terrorism legislation.

Germany reevaluated their immigration and terrorism laws when it was revealed several of the 9/11 attackers had lived in Hamburg, Germany prior to the attacks. A legal loophole was removed that allowed terrorists to live and raise money in Germany. Also, the country's law enforcement modified their communication tactics.

One of the most notable security measures enacted by the United States was the Transportation Security Administration (TSA) which is an airport security measure implemented to inspect passengers and luggage. The United States Marshals also assigned an agent, known as a sky or air marshal to every domestic flight.

Once the attacks were confirmed to have committed and orchestrated by Al-Qaeda and Osama bin Laden and more information came to light, this led to the most prominent aftermath of the 9/11 attacks which is still being fought today...the War in Afghanistan and the War on Terror.

# War in Afghanistan and Iraq

A month after the attacks, President George W. Bush demanded that the Taliban surrender Osama bin Laden and disband Al-Qaeda. The United Nations had bin Laden on their wanted list since 1999.

The Taliban responded by declining to extradite bin Laden unless the United States provided evidence of bin Laden's involvement. Other Al-Qaeda members were also wanted by the US, which the Taliban also declined to extradite.

Due to the Taliban not cooperating, the United States launched Operation Enduring Freedom and invaded Afghanistan with the help of the United Kingdom. Other countries in NATO lent aid in the efforts as well.

The United States and other countries soon occupied Afghanistan. The US built military bases in major cities across the country. The US military and other forces drove the Taliban from power. Although most of the Taliban and Al-Qaeda members were not captured, they did flee to Pakistan and other neighboring countries.

The United Nations authorized the International Security Assistance Force (ISAF) in order to secure citizens of Kabul. Until 2003, the Taliban had lost the majority of their control in Afghanistan.

The Taliban leader, Mullah Omar reorganized and launched a counter attack. In groups of 50 or more, the Taliban launched attacks on US military outposts using rocket missiles and improvised explosive devices.

In September 2002, the Taliban launched an insurgency and began jihad recruitment in both Afghanistan and Pakistan. Mobile Taliban training camps were set up for the recruits and trained in jihad and guerrilla warfare.

The Pakistani military failed in defending the country against the uprising of the Taliban. Instead, many Pakistani's joined and funded the Taliban. The Pakistan Taliban, also known as TTP, operate mainly near the border of Afghanistan, which has very little government.

The Pakistani Taliban is most well-known for the 2012 shooting of then-14-year old Malala Youzafazi as well as the Peshawar school attack, which killed 145 people. 132 of those were children.

This offshoot of the Taliban is focused on insurgency against the Pakistani government to overthrow current leaders, take over, and rule the country under Sharia Law.

They reject democracy and are against Western-style education and the employment of women. The TTP's primary goal is to take over the Pakistani government and force the country to follow extremely conservative Islam.

Mullah Omar named a leadership council and divided Taliban control into five different zones in Afghanistan. In 2003, the US launched Operation Mongoose after a Taliban group attacked. The military strike resulted in 18 Taliban fatalities.

In the summer of 2003, Taliban attacks continued to increase. Hundreds of Afghani citizens, humanitarian aid workers and both US and British soldiers were killed in the Taliban attacks.

Thousands of Taliban fighters were soon striking Afghanistan and building up resistance against the US over 200 Afghani police were killed in August 2003.

In 2005, the Afghan government with support of the US military launched a counter strike attack on the Taliban, which resulted in the Taliban forces being driven out and having at least 124 members killed.

In 2003, while the war in Afghanistan was still raging, the US along with the UK, Australia, Italy, Spain, Denmark, and Poland invaded Iraq. According to then UK Prime Minister Tony Blair, the purpose in invading Iraq was "to disarm Iraq of weapons of mass destruction, to end Saddam Hussein's support for terrorism, and to free the Iraqi people."

Other world leaders felt Iraq was detrimental to world peace due to Iraq possessing nuclear weapons. However, it was proven that the weapon's powers had expired by the International Atomic Energy Agency.

The invasion of Iraq was a highly controversial and protested event. Many felt the invasion was unjustified for many reasons and felt it was only to obtain Iraq's rich oil resources as American troops had started to occupy Iraq in 2002 before the invasion.

Then Secretary of State Colin Powell presented evidence of, "a computer generated image of a mobile biological weapons lab, which supposedly linked Saddam Hussein to Al-Qaeda."

However, there was no concrete evidence linking Saddam Hussein to Al-Qaeda or Osama bin Laden. A representative from the head of Iraqi intelligence, General Tahir Jalil Habbush al-Tikriti contacted former CIA director and terrorism consult to the US government, Vincent Cannistraro. The Iraqi general stated Saddam Hussein knew there was a movement to link him to the 9/11 attacks and to prove Iraq possessed nuclear weapons.

Vincent Cannistraro stated that "the Iraqis were prepared to satisfy these concerns. I reported the conversation to senior levels of the state department and I was told to stand aside and they would handle it," and that the Bush Administration rejected the offers because it allowed Hussein to remain in power.

The United Nations offered Iraq a deal, Security Council Resolution 1441 which offered Saddam Hussein a way to "comply with disarmament obligations." The Resolution stated Iraq was in breach of a United Nations ceasefire contract.

Other world leaders were against the American invasion of Iraq and seemed to reach a more diplomatic approach. In October 2002, Congress passed "Iraq Resolution," which allowed the President to "use any means necessary" against Iraq to overthrow Hussein.

Iraqi government officials continued to claim they had no weapons of mass destruction and continued to comply with the demands of the United Nations.

After Saddam Hussein passed a deadline set in place by the United States to leave Iraq, the armies struck and began the invasion. Hussein had gone into hiding and was found in a six-to-eight-foot deep hole. Troops were able to overthrow the Hussein regime. The conflict officially ended on May 1, 2003, after capturing the country's major cities.

Hussein was captured and stood trial for crimes including mass killings. He was found guilty of crimes against humanity and was executed by hanging on December 30,

2006. No evidence of nuclear weapons or Iraq's involvement in 9/11 was ever found.

While two wars were happening simultaneously, the Taliban and Al-Qaeda continued to gain momentum in Afghanistan and launch counterstrikes. These attacks continued to increase throughout the summer of 2003 for the continuing years.

Eventually, combined military forces pushed most of the Taliban forces out. In 2006, A special operation spearheaded by Italian special forces and airborne troopers attacked a Taliban base killing 70 members.

Intelligence officials estimated 10,000 Taliban fighters were present in Afghanistan and actively attacking. Out of these 10,000 an estimated 2,000-3,000 were full-time insurgents. Many of these individuals were young Afghans who felt as if they were fighting against American and other military forces invading and occupying their country by joining the Taliban and sacrificing themselves via suicide bombings.

Recruits from other countries such as Pakistan, Uzbekistan, Chechnya also joined the Taliban fighters. These fighters from outside Afghanistan were reportedly much more violent and better versed in bomb creation than the Afghan fighters.

The influx of fighters from neighboring countries gave the Taliban more strength than in previous years. In 2007, after American forces killed a top-ranking Taliban militant, an ambush attack against American forces resulted in 100 deaths of US soldiers. This made 2007 the deadliest year for Americans in Afghanistan.

The invasion of Afghanistan and the following war was the first in history to use drones and drone strikes as weaponry. The use of drones versus manpower has been both deadly and has saved the lives of military personnel previously responsible for managing strikes.

However, drone strikes have been controversial as the death toll often includes civilians who are not intended targets. Many argue the unlawful killing of citizens via drones puts the US military and government at risk for criminal charges.

The CIA, who is responsible for launching drone attacks claim screening processes are using to determine where and who the drones strike.

The agency's counter terrorism division employees 10 lawyers who write briefs, justifying certain attacks. If the brief's argument is considered weak by the CIA, then the strike is denied. In 2009, it was reported predator drone strikes killed nine of Al-Qaeda's top 20 commanders. It is believed Osama bin Laden's son, Saad bin Laden was killed in a drone strike the same year.

The US military stated Al-Qaeda has been routed and become unorganized. The strikes have also caused members to turn against one another, thus leading to an inevitable collapse of the Taliban. These strikes continue today and are helping to eradicate both ISIS and remaining Taliban and Al-Qaeda members.

After 2013, suicide bombings by the Taliban increased. These suicide bombings, a form of terrorism have killed thousands including soldiers, government officials, and most commonly unarmed civilians.

In March 2014, the Taliban bombed a military bus in Kabul, raided a hotel restaurant, and shot Swedish radio journalist Nils Homer.

Despite the bombings, troops from both the United States and The United Kingdom began to withdraw from Afghanistan. These troops were replaced by government-contracted private security companies hired by the US and the United Nations. These companies are primarily made up of former military members from various countries.

On May 27, 2014, President Barack Obama announced the US would discontinue military operations in Afghanistan in December 2014. 9,800 were to remain in order to train Afghan forces on counterterrorism. The private security agencies also withdrew their forces later in the year.

On December 28, 2014, NATO officially ended military operations in Afghanistan. The US continued to have military presence.

The United Kingdom officially ended their operations with a ceremony at St. Paul's Cathedral on March 13, 2015. Around 500 U.K troops still remain in Afghanistan.

In 2015, the US contained to have a military hold in Afghanistan by conducting and increasing raids against remaining Taliban and Al-Qaeda members as well as ISIS. Russia also opened its borders to allow for supplies and military to be delivered into Afghanistan.

In late 2016, the United States only had 8,400 troops left in Afghanistan. No more troops have been added. In February 2017, US President Donald Trump and Afghan President Ashraf Ghani discussed sending a few thousand troops back to Afghanistan to further the mission of wiping out the Taliban.

The War in Afghanistan, like 9/11 has had astronomical and immeasurable impacts on the world. The UN estimates that the Taliban killed several thousand civilians per year. A more official report conducted by the Watson Institute for International Studies Costs of War Project, 26,270 from 2001-2014.

Since 2001, more than 5.7 million refugees have returned to Afghanistan. 2.2 million of those individuals have remained refugees and settled elsewhere.

The United States was financially responsible for the vast majority of the War costs. In March 2011, US congressional research reported that since 2009 the Department of Defense's spending on the War had increased by 50%, skyrocketing from $4.4 billion a month to $6.7 billion a month.

The estimate for one soldier's deployment was over $1 million per year.

The high cost was one of the deciding factors for the United States to start withdrawing troops from Afghanistan. The total cost for the United Kingdom was $56.46 billion.

The US occupation and invasion of Afghanistan was a relief to many citizens who wanted the Taliban removed from their country. A 2006 survey showed 83% of

Afghans had a favorable view of the US military in their country.

Many citizens had anti-Taliban sentiments and were grateful for the intervention. Another survey conducted in 2015 found that more Afghans blame the Taliban for violence in their country than the United States.

The violence, civil unrest, and terrorist attacks led to the United States helping the country of Afghanistan for the better. Along with helping to remove the majority of the Taliban, the presence of the US army and NATO helped establish much-needed services and security in Afghanistan.

A policy implemented by the US allowed for the restructuring of the Afghan National Army. The policy helped the Afghan Army grow from 134,000 soldiers in October 2010 to 171,000 by 2011. The increase of troops led to the withdrawal of US and UK troops as well as established a standing army to continue the fight against the Taliban.

Within the Afghan National Army, there was an epidemic of insider attacks. These also existed within with Afghan National Police, which the US also helped form and train.

These attacks were led by Taliban members or sympathizers who infiltrated the army and police forces by joining both groups and launching attacks from within.

In 2011, there were 21 insider attacks from Taliban members and sympathizers resulting in 35 fatalities. In 2012, 46 more attacks followed with a death toll of 63. A US general was killed in another insider attack in 2014. Insider attacks and infiltration have greatly diminished since combat operations have ceased. The last reported insider attack by the Taliban was in 2014.

Along with setting up the Afghan National Army and police force, the US established much-needed health care facilities. With partnership from the Afghan government and the US Agency for International Development, the healthcare system in Afghanistan has been completely overhauled for the better.

As of 2002, before the healthcare initiative began Afghanistan had one the lowest life expectancy rates in the world. Since 2008, more than 57 percent of Afghans now live within one hour of a health facility, compared to 9 percent as of 2002. A focus on vital women's healthcare was also established which decreased the infant and child mortality rate.

Public education in Afghanistan was also furthered during the occupation. The enrollment of students in Afghan public schools increased from 1.2 million to 8.2 million from 2001 to 2015. 3.2 million of those students were girls.

One of the most widely felt impacts of the war and occupation in Afghanistan was the opium drug trade. By 2000 Afghanistan produced an estimated 75 percent of the world's opium supply. The same year, 3,276 tons were produced from 203,050 acres.

The key ingredient in heroin, which is now a serious drug epidemic in many parts of the world once accounted for the vast majority of the Taliban's income. In a New York Times article, Wahidullah Sabawoon, Finance Minister of the United Front, estimated the Taliban spent an equivalent of $300 million a year on war with funds from the opium drug trade.

Then Taliban leader Mullah Omar limited the production of opium as a tactic to raise prices and increase profits. The opium harvests in 1999 and 2000 were some of the largest and most profitable for the Taliban even with the decreased crop.

It is believed many of these funds earned from these harvests were used to fund the planning and execution of the 9/11 attacks. In the days after 9/11, Mullah Omar called for opium production to increase back to usual amounts.

The increased production led to Afghanistan producing 90 percent of the world's opium supply in 2005. The majority of this opium was made into heroin and sold in Europe and Russia.

A BBC report from 2009 stated that a UN study concluded that the Taliban's opium farms are worth $65 billion used to fund terrorism on a global scale. The same UN reports find that these drugs made from the Taliban's products result in 100,000 deaths per year.

The increase of heroin via the opium grown and disturbed by the Taliban can be directly linked to the ever-growing heroin epidemic across the world. This has not only linked the Taliban to hundreds of thousands of death via their violence but from their drug trafficking.

United States military forces and operations in Afghanistan have not completely ceased since 2001 although the war has significantly subsided. There has been no official end for the United States. The much-awaited end to the longest war in US is not set. As long as there is active terrorism, ISIS, Al-Qaeda, and other forces, there will be no end.

# The Conspiracies

Along with the entire world changing due to a mass terrorist attack and thousands of deaths, 9/11 ushered in many conspiracies. These conspiracies stemmed from the fear, anxiety, and uncertainty that were universally felt after the attacks.

If a small group of people could hijack four airplanes, send them flying into buildings, spread fear across the world, and have a war started due to their actions, what else was possible?

These theories attempt to find answers to the questions that were left unanswered. However, most conspiracy theories, especially those that relate to the 9/11 attacks and the war that followed tend to be particularly outlandish.

This could be due to a variety of factors. For starters, the events on 9/11 and what transpired from those events were unlike anything else the world had seen. It makes sense from that standpoint for shock and awe to take over and allow our imaginations to run wild as to what could possibly be next.

Technology was also a major factor in 9/11. In a few short years, technology has evolved so much that if 9/11 were to happen today, the aftermath could have been very different as we are so constantly connected that these conspiracies and other false information can spread very fast.

The Internet is a hotbed of these 9/11 conspiracies which have yet to die down despite the events occurring 16 years ago. Simply not enough time has passed to stop the interest and wondering. Also, the fact the events of 9/11 are still impacting the entire world doesn't help calm these theories.

The majority of these theories started circulating via the Internet soon after 9/11. Websites like YouTube, Reddit, Facebook, and now-called fake news sites have only led to more theories being developed and spread.

Mainly, the concept of conspiracy theories can be viewed as fun entertainment and to some, a look into the bizarre. On the other hand, sometimes these theories and those who believe and spread them can lead to fear and anxiety.

Conspiracy theories were once viewed as being obscure and of little merit. In recent years, the concept of conspiracy theories has entered from the dark corners of bookshelves and the Internet and into mainstream media. The media has recently begun using conspiracy theories to spread propaganda to gain power.

The prevalence of rampant conspiracy theories is not only rooted in our anxieties but by excitement of learning something new, or feeling superiority over believing in knowledge not everyone has. Psychology Today reports conspiracy theories, learning about and creating/spreading them leads to an adrenaline rush that can be addictive.

A study conducted in 2016 by Chapman University sociologist, Christopher Bader, found that 54.3 percent of participants believed the government is withholding information about the 9/11 attacks.

There are many 9/11 conspiracies, some of which present an interesting and compelling argument backed by science and evidence. Others are not so compelling and do not provide any scientifically backed evidence.

The most prevalent 9/11 conspiracy theory is perhaps the most obvious; the attacks were planned and executed by the United States government as a false flag operation in order to lead the country into a war with Afghanistan and Iraq.

Probably the second most common theory and the most believable based on numerous pieces of evidence is that the United States government knew the attacks were coming, but let it happen in order to go to war.

Compared to all the other theories, some of which are outlandish, this one actually has evidence. The FBI, CIA, and NSA warnings as well as the August 6, 2001, Presidential Daily Briefing all proves that there were Taliban terrorist attacks headed to the United States.

In relation to the government not stopping the attacks, those who buy into the theory also believe on 9/11 then Vice President Dick Cheney ordered the military to stand down and not shoot down or intercept the hijacked planes.

This was proven false as fighter jets did not have time to intercept the plane. There are also records of Dick Cheney ordering any known hijacked plane to be shot down, although no orders were ever given due to Flight 93 already having crashed in Shanksville, Pennsylvania.

The reasoning behind a government wanting their own country to go to war could be that leaders (in this case, President George W. Bush) tend to be remembered more fondly. Also, war often leads to an economic boost. US presidents in office when the economy is stable or performing above average are also celebrated.

A false flag operation historically evolved from naval ships flying under another country's flag in order to confuse enemy ships. The term has recently evolved into meaning an event planned by a government or group and blamed on another, such as the Taliban or Al-Qaeda.

This particular theory is also tied into another commonly believed theory that the planes were actually missiles launched by the US military. This theory is easily disproven as video evidence proves otherwise.

The 9/11 Commission Report as well as studies conducted by FEMA, and the National Institute of Standards and Technology all prove the attacks were in fact planned and executed by Al-Qaeda. Most conspiracy theorists refute these studies and claim they were altered by the government to cover up the truth.

The missile theory is mainly applied to the attack on the Pentagon but has been linked to all three attack sites. The reasoning behind the Pentagon having been attacked with a missile, according to theorists is that the damage was not significant enough to have been done by a commercial airliner. This idea has also been disproven based on video, eyewitness, and physical evidence.

The missile theory can be traced back to a television journalist who witnessed the attacks and made a comment about the plane hitting the second tower not having any windows. The journalists then suggested that perhaps it was a missile and not a plane hitting the building.

As with the missile theory and others, they can usually be traced back to something that was said on 9/11 by reporters and witnesses and/or observations made in the following weeks.

Surprisingly, some of the first 9/11 theories originated in Europe, not the United States. The "inside job" and false flag theory was presented by a French researcher for a thesis being written for the French National Centre for Scientific Research only a week after the attacks.

Six months later, a French book about 9/11, "L'Effroyable Imposture" was a bestseller. When the book was eventually published in English under the title "9/11: The Big Lie" it received little acclaim and sales.

It is now one of the main sources used by theorists and those who are referred to as "truthers" or "9/11 truthers." These individuals seek to prove various conspiracies and that the United States government planned and carried out the attacks. They believe the conspiracies are "the truth".

Other books about conspiracies related to the attacks were soon published in Germany and England. These theories were soon spreading to the United States but were not as popular as they are now until about 2004.

Americans believed the theories originating in Europe were a product of "Anti-Americanism." On November 10, 2001, in an address to the United Nations, President George W. Bush dismissed the "outrageous conspiracy theories [...] that attempt to shift the blame away from the terrorists, themselves, away from the guilty."

The rise of the conspiracy theories related to 9/11 is believed to have been attributed to the growing animosity towards the Bush Administration and the War in Iraq. The newly re-elected George W. Bush was facing more criticism than ever in 2004 when these theories started emerging. The theories that the attacks were ignored by the government came to a head when the August 6, 2001, President Daily Brief was published in a newspaper.

Another common theory is that the collapse of both World Trade Center towers was a result of bombs planted in the building as a result of the government conducting the attacks so the building would be sure to collapse. During investigations and rescue missions when the fires in the World Trade Center were fully extinguished showed no evidence of any explosives in the debris.

The bomb theory correlates to another popular theory about the structural integrity of the World Trade Center towers themselves. Many believe that the lightweight aluminum of the commercial planes would have not been powerful enough to either cause the buildings to collapse and burn.

While this thought does hold some credence, when the speed at which the planes were flying and the vast amounts of jet fuel present are factored in the answer becomes obvious.

All of the flights hijacked on 9/11 were scheduled to fly nonstop across the country from the East Coast. The full tanks of jet fuel along with flammable materials inside the

Twin Towers as well as the Pentagon it was proven that the fuel caused the fires that led to the collapse of the Twin Towers.

Theorists argue this with evidence no other skyscraper has collapsed simply due to a fire and believe that bombs were planted or the collapse was due to rigged explosives for a staged demolition.

According to the BBC, scientists who believe in this theory have claimed to have a sample of dust from the Twin Towers. These scientists reported the materials possessed, "thermitic material which reacts violently when heated up," that points to explosives in the building.

National Institute of Standards and Technology conducted a three-year study and investigation into the collapse of the World Trade Center. Their findings showed the buildings collapsed due to "uncontrolled fires" in the North Tower. The North Tower fire burned for a total of seven hours.

If explosives had been involved, noise would have been a factor in identifying them. Fires and demolition from explosives leave behind different evidence. The "thermitic material" that was supposedly found by the scientists was concluded to be paint primer from the walls inside the Twin Towers.

The United States Geological Survey conducted a story on the 1,200,000 tons of material that was destroyed during the collapse of the Twin Towers. Their findings concluded minerals were present in the debris and dust, but no thermite or explosives were ever found.

A group called Architects & Engineers for 9/11 Truth, who go by AE911Truth have formed a non-profit in order to disprove government reports about the collapse of the Twin Towers and the damage at the Pentagon.

The group, headed by a member of the American Institute of Architects believes in the theory of controlled demolition and planted bombs. The mission of the group is to get Congress to invest in an independent investigation of the attacks and the collapse of the Twin Towers.

What many refer to as the "forgotten attack or plane," Flight 93 was also believed to have shot down by missiles. Some believe the military knew the plane was hijacked and shot it down, or that the plane was a missile heading for another target. Some believe Flight 93 was shot down because the passengers learned of the government's plan to cover up their involvement in the attacks.

Theorists believe the missile disintegrated the plane and scattered debris over a large area, which is why the crash site seemed small. In reality, the wind was responsible for carrying pieces of the lightweight plane a mere mile. While others claim that the plane's engine was found miles away from the crash site.

The claim about the engine was proven incorrect as it was later found 300 yards from the main crash site. An airline accident expert and investigator found the position of the engine to be conclusive with a plane crashing at 500 mph or more, which the plane was traveling.

The cockpit voice recorder in Flight 93 was not destroyed upon impact and proves the passenger revolt and that the hijackers had crashed the plane. This is a vital piece of evidence in the investigations of the crashes and hijackings.

Much like other theories, this one can be tied back to a local coroner, Wally Miller who made a remark about the site not having any bodies present at the scene. It was later found Miller was unaware of the plane crash and once he realized what had happened, he claimed there would have to be a large funeral.

The attack on the Pentagon presented a similar situation. These theories particularly relating to the Pentagon and the Flight 93 crash tend to focus more on the missile belief and the lack of wreckage more so than the World Trade Center.

In comparison, the Pentagon and Flight 93 were much smaller in scale than two skyscrapers falling and burning at the same time. The damage and death tolls would naturally be smaller at the other sites as they are much smaller in surface area and square footage than the Twin Towers.

On the day of 9/11, much confusion and misinformation was circulating within the news media that the first footage of the Pentagon attack appeared not to show much damage.

With the comparing size scales in consideration, the missile theories seem more probably when tied to the Pentagon and Flight 93. Airplane wreckage as well as the black box recordings from both flights proves the missile theory false.

Flight 93 seems to still be more of a mystery than the other hijacked flights as many of the theories and speculation revolve around that particular flight. This could be because it was the last attack that took place on 9/11 and that the Pentagon and World Trade Center received more media attention simply because they happened first. Also, the fact the black box was not destroyed leaving behind evidence leads to more speculation.

One of the many questions non-truthers and non-theorists often come up with concerns the bodies of the deceased passengers. Theorists who believe the missile theory will argue that the passengers were not real, but were actors.

Others tend to follow the theory that the "faked" plane crash victims were either murdered by the government and had their bodies destroyed, or were relocated in the style of the Witness Protection Program to cover up the government involvement.

A Shanksville, Pennsylvania woman, Valencia McClatchey took the only known photograph of the mushroom cloud explosion from the Flight 93 crash. She says she has been harassed for years by conspiracy theorists who claim she faked the photo. The FBI and the Smithsonian have both examined the photo and have proven it is authentic.

In the documentary film, loose Change 9/11: An American Coup, director and 9/11 theorists Dylan Avery points to Flight 93 having landed in Cleveland. Avery believes another plane was substituted in for Flight 93 by the government to stage the crash and hijacking.

However, the flight that actually did land in Cleveland was Delta Flight 1989 which had been suspected of being hijacked as well.

Some also believe the black boxes from all four flights were kept secret to hide government involvement or evidence of explosives. The only black box left audible was from Flight 93. This is the only recorded evidence from any of the flights.

Along with the black boxes in the planes, many passengers called their relatives from the flights on cellphones. Some of these calls were recorded and saved by family members.

Theorists have mounted evidence that these phone calls were fake. This seems extremely heartless and callous considering the events of the day and the number of people who lost their lives.

One of these supposedly faked phone calls was from a Flight 93 attendant, CeeCee Lyles. In a voicemail left to her husband, supposedly another female voice is heard saying, "you did great," meaning Lyles was being given a script. The most logical explanation of this comment could be that Lyles was sitting next to a woman on the plane who offered her encouragement.

Theorists also point to voice morphing and actors having portrayed the passengers/victims. Many feel as if the individuals making the phone calls lacked emotion, which theorists claim are actors.

The theory is based on the fact that at the time, cell phones could not be used in aircraft due to high altitudes. This was quickly disproven.

One odd piece of evidence in pointing to the faked phone calls was a recording of a call made by Flight 93 passenger Mark Bingham to his mother. During the call, he refers to himself by his full name, saying, "Hi Mom, this is Mark Bingham."

Many point this out as being strange. Why would a child have to say their full name to their own mother? While this is an odd detail, Mark's mother was reported to have a different last name. His mother released the phone call and said he had no doubt it was her son, Mark and seemed baffled as to why he would use his full name.

Despite the outlandish and improbable theories, there is one that seems legitimate; insider trading the day before the attacks. In the weeks leading up to 9/11, both the stocks for United and American Airlines had what has been labeled "extraordinary" put options.

A put option is when an owner of a stock sells an asset at a specified price by a predetermined date. These stock sales point to insiders knowing about the attacks and profiting from them by selling the stock by the date of the attacks.

Insurance companies also experienced increased stock trading right before the attacks as well. Travelers Insurance, owned by Citigroup was estimated to pay $500 million in claims from the World Trade Center attacks.

Travelers experienced 45 times the normal trading volume during the three trading days before the attacks and only for options that profit if the stock falls before $40 per share. Shares in Citigroup decreased to $38.09. Morgan Stanley, which then occupied 22 floors of the World Trade Center, experienced the same phenomena.

It has been well-documented that an unknown individual made $5 million from buying and selling airline stocks in the days leading up to the attacks.

The insider trading was addressed and investigated during the 9/11 Commission Report found that the FBI and the Securities and Exchange Commission reported no evidence of insider trader or that anyone knew about the attacks ahead of time.

Theories about the hijackers started circulating once their names were released to the public. Due to the confusion and speculation about the attacks, when the BBC published the names of who they believed to be the hijackers, many claimed they were still alive. This gave theorists even more reason to believe the attacks were faked.

The BBC later explained that many of the hijackers had common Arabic and Islamic names which led to the confusion and mistaken identities. Once the FBI released photographs of the hijackers, the confusion was cleared up.

The 9/11 Commission later reported that sixteen out of the nineteen hijackers were let into the United States illegally due to errors in the visas and passports. The Commission head, Thomas Kean claimed if half the hijackers had been stopped, there never would have been a plot.

This also ties back to the communication issues between the FBI and CIA and sharing intelligence as two of the hijackers, Khalid al

Mihdhar and Nawaf al Hazmi were known to the CIA as Al-Qaeda members.

A theory involving Israel also evolved in the years after 9/11 based on the conflict in the country with Palestine. On the day of the attacks, two Israeli men were spotted filming the New York City skyline for several minutes before the first plane hit.

Witnesses report these two men were "acting strangely" and did not show shock or react appropriately when the planes struck the Twin Towers.

The Anti-Defamation League was the first to document the theory stating that Israel was involved in some way and/or planned the attacks and blamed Al-Qaeda. The theory suggests Israel attacked the United States as a way to get the US to attack Israeli enemies, or to divert media and government attention away from the conflict with Palestine, to help Zionists take power over world affairs, and to convince Americans to support Israel.

Many support this theory based on the fact that there were very little Jews killed in the attacks in correlation to the total number of Jews living in New York City at the time.

Some believe that Jewish employees were told about the attacks ahead of time and were told to skip work on 9/11, which according to theorists who buy into this theory led to no Jewish deaths at the World Trade Center.

In reality, it was estimated anywhere from 270 to 400 Jews were killed in the World Trade Center. It is estimated that around 4,000 Jewish people called into and/or skipped work in New York City on 9/11.

This is backed up by a report aired on a Lebanese news channel on September 17, 2001. This news report is said to have used a September 12, 2001, newspaper article from The Jerusalem Post which said that The Jerusalem Foreign Ministry received the names of 4,000 Israelis who were believed to have been in the area near the World Trade Center and the Pentagon on 9/11. A total of five Israeli citizens died in the attacks.

The Anti-Defamation League published another report in 2003 attacking "hateful conspiracy theories" relating to Jewish and Israeli involvement in 9/11.

Some theorists refute this and believe the attacks were carried out by Jews to gain world domination, for their own financial gain, and for the United States to exhaust their own military resources to attack Middle Eastern enemies.

Increased anti-Semitic theories became very common after the attacks, according to a former United Nations diplomat.

Saudi Arabia was also implicated in being involved in the attacks as well. A British investigative journalist claimed the Saudi Royal Family provided financial support to the hijackers and that the Bush

Administration covered this up to protect their own interests in Saudi Arabia.

In 2011, an individual at the famous London, England insurance agency, Lloyd's, began legal proceedings against Saudi Arabia demanding repayment of the 136 million pounds the company paid out to victims of the 9/11 attacks.

Members of the Saudi Royal Family as well as many banks and charities in Saudi Arabia have been accused of being Al-Qaeda agents by funding terrorism and "encouraged anti-Western sentiment."

Compared to other theories and speculation, potential Saudi Arabian involvement in the 9/11 attacks does hold some credence.

Fifteen out of nineteen of the hijackers were from Saudi Arabia, as was Osama bin Laden.

The bin Laden family was also very wealthy and had connections to the Saudi Royal Family. Some of the hijackers had connections in the Saudi Arabian government. The passports of some of the hijackers were also believed to have tampered with by the Saudi government to allow them and easier entry into the United States.

It was also reported that the Saudi Arabian government and royal family was known to fear Al-Qaeda, and worried the terrorist group would attempt to overthrow their government. In response, the Saudi Arabian government funded Al-Qaeda to keep them the peace between the two groups.

In 2016, a federal lawsuit filed in Manhattan against Saudi Arabia by some of the families of 9/11 victims. The suit seeks to hold Saudi Arabia responsible for the attacks.

The suit documents how the Saudi government helped fund, train, and tampered with passports to allow the fifteen Saudi hijackers into the United States.

Also in 2016, declassified documents were released showing a link between the Saudi government, the hijackers, and Al-Qaeda. The Bush Administration refused to disclose the documents due to national security.

In September 2016, Congress passed the Justice against Sponsors of Terrorism Act which allows for Americans to take legal action against countries whose citizens have conducted terrorist attacks. President Obama vetoed the bill and it was quickly overridden by Congress. This was the first and only presidential veto override in Obama's administration.

Many believe the bill was passed to directly target Saudi Arabia. The passing of Justice against Sponsors of Terrorism Act was one of the rare occasions in which House Democrats and Republicans agreed on a bill.

When the bill was first presented, lawmakers feared it would put the United States at risk due to backlash from other countries. They also feared a similar law could be passed elsewhere.

The bill has created some controversy in Saudi Arabia When the bill was first introduced in 2009, the Saudi government threatened to sell $750 billion worth of US Treasury securities and other US-related assets. Economists assured the US government that Saudi Arabia could not afford to sell the assets and securities without "crippling the kingdom's economy."

Saudi Arabia also recently made headlines for not being included in President Donald Trump's controversial travel ban on primarily Muslim countries. Americans who support the travel ban feel Saudi Arabia should be included due to the connections to

9/11 and the hijackers. It is believed the country is not included in the travel ban due to Donald Trump's personal business dealings in the country.

For all the 9/11 theories that do some related evidence, no matter how small and easily arguable there is one theory that is perhaps the most outlandish; the hologram theory.

The hologram theory, also known as the no-planes theory states that the attacks were caused by missiles and that holograms were used to project the image of a plane to the world.

One of the most prominent proponents of the hologram theories is former Labor Department chief economist, Morgan

Reynolds. Reynolds claims it was impossible that the Boeing planes could have caused the steel frames of the Twin Towers to collapse. He insists that digital composting was sued to make the missiles appear to be planes.

Reynolds claims that his theory is the truth and that he knows the truth based on his position in the Bush Administration. Many theorists and 9/11 truthers refute the hologram theory, which is very controversial in some truther groups. Some group message boards have banned any mention of the hologram/no-plane theory. There has even been violence threatened at protests by theorists from both sides.

# Close

The terrorist attacks on September 11, 2001, forever changed the world and modern society. The attacks have resulted in immeasurable impacts on everything from security, air travel, immigration, and more.

On what the world thought was going to be a normal day, turned into the most infamous date in human history. The events of 9/11 prove we never know what is around the corner waiting for us.

The recent memories of the attacks, the wars, and events that followed still live on in minds around the world.

Made in the USA
San Bernardino, CA
27 December 2019